THE FAMILY
CLASSICS
Diabetes Cookbook

Over **140** Favorite Recipes from the pages of *Diabetes Forecast* Magazine

American
Diabetes
Association®

Director, Book Publishing, Abe Ogden; Managing Editor, Greg Guthrie; Acquisitions Editor, Rebekah Renshaw; Editor, Rebekah Renshaw; Production Manager, Melissa Sprott; Composition and Cover Design, pixiedesign, llc; Recipe Developer, Robyn Webb; Photographer, Taran Z; Printer, RR Donnelley.

Printed in the United States of America

1 3 5 7 9 10 8 6 4 2

The suggestions and information contained in this publication are generally consistent with the Clinical Practice Recommendations and other policies of the American Diabetes Association, but they do not represent the policy or position of the Association or any of its boards or committees. Reasonable steps have been taken to ensure the accuracy of the information presented. However, the American Diabetes Association cannot ensure the safety or efficacy of any product or service described in this publication. Individuals are advised to consult a physician or other appropriate health care professional before undertaking any diet or exercise program or taking any medication referred to in this publication. Professionals must use and apply their own professional judgment, experience, and training and should not rely solely on the information contained in this publication before prescribing any diet, exercise, or medication. The American Diabetes Association—its officers, directors, employees, volunteers, and members—assumes no responsibility or liability for personal or other injury, loss, or damage that may result from the suggestions or information in this publication.

∞ The paper in this publication meets the requirements of the ANSI Standard Z39.48-1992 (permanence of paper).

ADA titles may be purchased for business or promotional use or for special sales. To purchase more than 50 copies of this book at a discount, or for custom editions of this book with your logo, contact the American Diabetes Association at the address below, at booksales@diabetes.org, or by calling 703-299-2046.

American Diabetes Association
1701 North Beauregard Street
Alexandria, Virginia 22311
DOI: 10.2337/9781580404846

Library of Congress Cataloging-in-Publication Data

The family classics diabetes cookbook : over 140 favorite recipes from the pages of diabetes forecast magazine / American Diabetes Association.

  p. cm.

  Includes bibliographical references and index.

  ISBN 978-1-58040-484-6 (pbk.)

  1. Diabetes--Diet therapy--Recipes. I. American Diabetes Association.

  RC662.F34 2012

  641.5'6314--dc23

             2012031985

TABLE OF CONTENTS

190   PORK/BEEF

204   PASTA

216   CASSEROLES

ACKNOWLEDGMENTS

THE AMERICAN DIABETES ASSOCIATION THANKS ROBYN WEBB
FOR THE RECIPES DEVELOPED FOR THIS PUBLICATION,
AS WELL AS PHOTOGRAPHER TARAN Z FOR THE AMAZING
FOOD SHOTS THROUGHOUT THIS COOKBOOK.

COOKING 101

BUILDING THE PERFECT PANTRY SYSTEM

Wouldn't it be terrific if you could count on being able to make a healthy and delicious meal at a moment's notice—and without an extra run to the supermarket? With a properly stocked kitchen, you should be able to do just that. Our pantry system lists about three dozen items that you should keep on hand at all times. We've divided them into **Brilliant Basics** (mainly canned staples), **Cold Comforts** (food kept in the refrigerator and freezer), and **Flavor Savers** (herbs and spices, but also salsa, mustard, and the like).

Once you have them, you'll come to understand how versatile these ingredients are. Suddenly, broth is more than just a soup when you use it in place of water to cook grains and pasta. Canned tomatoes become a base for homemade pasta sauce or soup, or a topping for grilled chicken breast. Salsa is great as a dip, but you can also top a grilled fish fillet with it, or use it as a quickie sauce for cooked vegetables. Fresh lemon and lime juice can be sprinkled over cooked vegetables, mixed into salad dressings, or squeezed into a glass of ice-cold water. No-sugar-added preserves become part of a glaze for pan-seared meat, chicken, or fish, or, melted down, they're a syrup for pancakes, waffles, or French toast.

A good pantry will equip you to try new recipes, since these basic items are the building blocks of many, many dishes. And remember: A pantry is a work in progress. For example, once you have the basic vinegars on hand, you might decide to branch out to include more exotic types such as champagne vinegar. Similarly, extra-virgin olive oil is easy to find, but you could add walnut or macadamia nut oil to your collection for a different kind of flavor.

There's an art to building a great working pantry, once you have the right blueprint.

THE LIST

Brilliant Basics:

Canned beans | Types that are good to have on hand include black, pinto, garbanzo (chickpea), and red kidney beans. Choose lower-sodium when possible. Leftover beans can be refrigerated, covered, for 2 to 3 days.

Canned tuna | in water, not oil. Any leftover can be stored in the refrigerator, tightly covered, for 1 to 2 days.

Brown rice | Store in an airtight container for up to a year. (Keeping a dried red chili pepper in the same container will repel mealy bugs.) Cooked rice can be refrigerated, covered, for up to a week.

Whole-grain pasta | at least one strand (linguini, spaghetti) and one shaped (penne, fusilli) pasta. Uncooked dried pasta can be kept in an airtight container for up to a year. If it develops white speckles, toss it. Cooked pasta can be refrigerated, covered, for up to 2 to 3 days.

Fat-free or low-fat reduced-sodium chicken and vegetable broth | Once opened, broth can be stored, sealed, in the refrigerator for about 1 to 2 weeks.

Fresh tomatoes | Store at room temperature. Once cut, wrap well in plastic and refrigerate for 1 to 2 days.

Canned whole and diced tomatoes | Refrigerate leftover canned tomatoes in an airtight container for 3 to 4 days or freeze for up to 4 to 5 months.

Tomato paste | Try to get the tube rather than the can; although the tube is slightly more expensive, leftover paste is more easily stored that way in the fridge.

Potatoes | sweet potatoes and white (Idaho/russet) potatoes. Buy hard potatoes with no bruising or splitting. White potatoes should not be green and should have no sprouting or eyes. Sweet potatoes' first sign of deterioration is shriveling and softness. Store both kinds for up to 2 weeks in a cool, dry bottom pantry shelf with good air circulation.

Cold Comforts:

Meat | skinless chicken breasts and thighs, boneless pork tenderloin, ground white-meat turkey, ground white-meat chicken, or lean ground beef (93 percent). Keep for only 1 to 2 days in the refrigerator and no more than 4 months in the freezer, tightly wrapped.

Frozen vegetables | broccoli, corn, spinach, peas, or a medley of these and others. Use within 4 months. Tightly seal unused portions.

Frozen stuffed pasta | tortellini and the like (whole wheat if you can find it). Use within 8 to 9 months.

Eggs (large) | Store in the coldest part of the refrigerator in the original carton for up to 3 weeks.

Lemons and limes | Use within 1 week for best freshness.

Fresh herbs | parsley, cilantro, mint, and dill. Bundle together with a rubber band and place in a glass of water. Cover loosely with a plastic bag. Store in the refrigerator for 2 to 3 days.

Fresh carrots | Store in the fridge's produce bin for up to 2 weeks, or until they begin to wither and become soft.

Fresh celery | Wrap loosely in a large plastic bag and place in the produce bin. It should keep for about 3 days.

Scallions | Purchase plump scallions that are not withered or beginning to yellow. Wrap in damp paper towels and keep refrigerated for up to 2 days.

Flavor Savers:

Vinegar | red wine, white wine, and balsamic. Use within 1 year.

Extra-virgin olive oil | Transfer to an opaque container (can also be refrigerated). Use within 6 to 7 months.

Lower-sodium or light soy sauce | Use within 1 year.

Dijon mustard | coarse or smooth. Use within 1 year. Once opened, store it in the refrigerator.

Salsa (in a jar) | Keep for 1 year in the pantry. Once opened, keep in the refrigerator for no more than 1 month.

Fresh onions and garlic | Keep in the bottom of the pantry in a container with good air circulation for 1 to 2 weeks. If they start to sprout, toss them.

Dried herbs and spices | basil, oregano, Italian blend, rosemary, cumin, ground cinnamon, chili powder (hot or mild), dried red chili flakes, ground cayenne, ground coriander, allspice, onion and garlic powders, ground paprika, black pepper (preferably whole peppercorns for grinding), and kosher or sea salt. Keep tightly sealed, away from light and heat; use within 1 year.

Capers | Use within 1 year. Once opened, store in the refrigerator for 2 months.

Black olives | Use within 1 year. Once opened, store in the refrigerator and use within a few weeks.

No-sugar-added preserves | Use within 1 year. Once opened, store in the refrigerator.

Plain bread crumbs | Store tightly covered and use within 1 year.

Sweeteners | Choose some combination of sugar, Splenda, stevia, honey, maple syrup, agave nectar, and brown sugar.

Wine | Avoid "cooking wines." Choose dry whites like pinot grigio or sauvignon blanc. For reds, you generally can't go wrong with merlot and Chianti. Once opened, use within a few days.

UP TO PAR

Want to run your home kitchen the way the professionals do? Then you need to keep what is known as a par. This is a running tally of all the food items you have in your kitchen. To establish one, you will need to figure out how often you use certain items, and how much of them. For example, if you use 3 cans of diced tomatoes a week, make sure you always have at least 4 to 6 on hand, so you never run out. It's an easy system that you can store on a computer, or just tack a sheet of paper on the inside of the pantry door to record your inventory. Keep it updated at all times, and you'll be able to make your favorite recipe whenever you want. Another tip: Write the date of purchase on food packages, so you'll know when it's time to dump them.

Now that you have your pantry fully stocked and ready to go, get out there and cook. For those who haven't spent much time in the kitchen (or those who just need a reminder), the section below provides How To tips for some of the trickier cooking techniques. Learn how to make perfect pasta, tips for how to cook and store fish, how to build a healthier casserole for your family, and tips for making your favorite grilled recipes perfect!

HOW TO MAKE FISH

If you're like most Americans, you probably don't eat as much fish as you could. Yes, we all know that it's generally one of the healthiest sources of protein, but the fussiness of preparing fish can be a major turnoff. Still, cooking fish doesn't have to be a special event. In fact, it can be one of the quickest meals to prepare. Here's a guide on how to buy fish, how to store it, and how to make it great. Chapter 8 has some great fish recipes that are perfect for trying out the tips below.

AT A GLANCE: FRESH FISH

- All fresh fish should have firm and springy flesh. If you're buying a whole fish, look for bright, clear eyes, red gills, and bright tight scales or shiny skin.

- Fresh filets or steaks should appear to be freshly cut, and not dried out or browning.

- Ask for your fish to be placed in a bag of ice for the trip home, no matter how close you live to the store. Remove the fish from its original wrapper, and rewrap in plastic wrap or a plastic bag. Place the rewrapped fish in a dish, cover with ice, and store in the refrigerator. Use within 24 hours.

Baking & Roasting

These are particularly good methods for cooking thick filets. To bake, add fish to a shallow pan along with wine, lemon juice, olive oil, and herbs and spices. Cook, uncovered, in a preheated oven at 350 degrees until just tender. (Roasting takes a higher oven temperature and a few minutes less cooking time.) Tip: Start checking for doneness halfway through your recipe's suggested cooking time. Insert the tines of a fork into the thickest part of the fish and lift up; if the fish is opaque inside, it's ready to eat. *Cooking time: 12 to 15 minutes.*

Broiling & Grilling

Fish steaks and thicker filets hold up best under the broiler or on the grill.

Brush them with oil before and during cooking. If the fish are small or a bit thin, you might want to use a separate fish griller basket that sits right on the grill. *Cooking time: 10 to 15 minutes.*

Panfrying

You can coat thin filets in whole-wheat bread crumbs, crushed seeds or nuts, flour, or a combination of any of these. The best fish for panfrying are lean filets such as flounder, perch, orange roughy, tilapia, and sole. Dip fish in a beaten egg or egg white first to coat with crumbs (for flour, no egg is needed). Heat a large skillet with a small amount of vegetable oil. Panfry fish, turning once. *Cooking time: 8 to 10 minutes.*

Poaching

In a skillet, cover fish filets or steaks in water, clam juice, chicken broth, white wine, or a combination of any of these. Add a few whole black peppercorns and slices of onion. Bring the liquid to a simmer, cover, and simmer for about 8 minutes per inch of thickness. Remove the fish with a slotted spoon. You can boil down the poaching liquid until it becomes syrupy and then pour it over the fish. Or discard the liquid, refrigerate the poached fish, and serve it cold with a chilled or room-temperature sauce like cucumber yogurt.

> **AT A GLANCE: FROZEN FISH**
>
> - There should be little or no odor to wrapped frozen fish. Look for solidly frozen flesh with clear color, free of ice crystals. Discoloration, a brownish tinge, or a covering of crystals indicates that the fish may have been thawed and refrozen.
>
> - Keep frozen fish in the freezer in the original wrapper; use immediately after thawing. Never thaw and refreeze fish, since this will cause moisture loss and changes in texture and flavor.
>
> - The best way to thaw frozen fish is to leave it in its wrapping and thaw it in the refrigerator or in a bowl of cold water. Thawing at room temperature can cause sogginess. Drain well and blot dry with paper towels before cooking.

HOW TO MAKE THE PERFECT PASTA

Pasta can be sorted into three main categories (leaving out the stuffed varieties, that is). Long noodles, like tagliatelle and cappellini, differ by diameter and shape: They can be flat, hollow, thin, or round. There are more than 100 known varieties of short pasta, familiar ones like rigatoni and fusilli but an array of other shapes, too, including francesine, cavatappi, and galletti. Little pastas are used mainly in soups, although they can also go nicely in salads. They include ditalini, mini farfalle, and alphabet pasta.

1. Choose a Noodle

First question: fresh or dry? It's mostly a matter of taste. Fresh pasta has a silky texture and a richer flavor than dry. It's well suited to delicate and smooth sauces, such as pesto. You'll want to cook and serve fresh pasta soon after buying (or making) it.

Dry pasta, on the other hand, retains its firmness when cooked. It's preferable for chunky sauces. The best dry pasta has a slightly rough texture. This indicates that the pasta was shaped using traditional bronze dies; sauces will adhere better to it. While it can be stored in a kitchen cabinet, you don't want to keep dry pasta more than a few months, since it will take on a stale taste.

2. Cook It Properly

When cooking pasta, you want to give your noodles a lot of water to move around in. A good rule of thumb is about 6 quarts of water in an 8-quart pot for 1 pound of pasta. Salt the water; otherwise your pasta will taste flat no matter how good your sauce is. (Not to fear: Most of that sodium will eventually end up down the drain.)

Once the salted water is at a full, rolling boil, add the pasta. Then bring it back quickly to another boil, and time the cooking from there. The best way to maintain the boiling temperature is to put the lid on the pot once you have added the noodles. If the pasta water is not maintained at a rapid boil, the pasta will cook faster on the outside and remain raw on the inside. It's also more likely to stick together. And don't even think of adding oil to the cooking water. Oil makes it more difficult for the sauce to adhere to the pasta.

Pasta is best when it's cooked al dente (Italian for "to the tooth"); there should be a slight resistance when you chew. You can also tell if it's al dente by its appearance: Cut it in half and you should see a white spot at the center. But if you are planning on further simmering cooked pasta in a sauce, then slightly undercook your pasta, so you can finish it to al dente in the saucepot.

3. Sauce It Well

While you want to drain the pasta thoroughly, resist the temptation to rinse it; the surface starch helps the sauce cling. But check your recipe before dumping the cooking water; it can come in handy for making some sauces, like **Creamy Cheese Sauce for Pasta** (page 209). Speaking of cheese: Refrain from automatically adding it to every pasta you eat. In Italy, cheese is used very selectively, and never in seafood sauces. For other dishes, it's best to just shave a small amount of flavorful hard cheese (say, Parmesan) on top of your plate.

A nice touch to finish: Warm the serving bowl you are going to serve the pasta in. The easiest way to do this is to pour some of the hot pasta cooking water into the bowl and let it sit for 30 seconds. Drain, and then add the noodles. Then take a moment to admire your work; pasta dishes should be served warm, not piping hot.

HOW TO CRAFT A HEALTHY CASSEROLE

There's nothing innately bad about the idea of a casserole: a savory one-pot entrée that can go directly from oven to dinner table. It's the traditional execution that's the problem, all that sloppy, gooey cheese and dense layers of refined carbs. So what can be done to rescue this retro favorite? We ventured into the kitchen to figure out how to keep the convenience of the casserole while ditching the extraneous fat and refined carbs. The result? Just like 1950s comfort food—updated for the 21st century.

1. Pack It In

One serious issue with old-fashioned casseroles is their reliance on fatty meats. You can get just as much flavor and far less saturated fat with 93 to 96 percent lean ground beef, lean cuts of poultry, or canned fish packed in water. (If you're sautéing meat, don't forget to drain off any fat before adding the other ingredients.) Or try subbing out half the meat for beans, which up the fiber and lower the overall fat content.

Casseroles traditionally combine that protein with a starch. Too often, however, that means white rice or white noodles. A simple switch to brown rice can give your dish a major nutritional boost. Or try different kinds of grains (below). For your vegetables, the classics work best: mild veggies like potatoes, green beans, broccoli, peas, onions, and carrots.

2. Sauce It Up

A casserole's sauce is what binds the protein and starch together. Usually, that means making a roux: butter and flour cooked with whole milk or cream, which adds a lot of unnecessary fat. Instead, you can use just a little flour with fat-free milk or low-fat or fat-free evaporated milk. Or no flour at all: In the **Cheesy Broccoli and Rice Casserole** (page 223), the starch released from the brown rice is what thickens the milk. Or, for something completely different, you can go fat free, as with the barbecue sauce in our **Biscuit and Hamburger Pie** (page 225).

The other treacherous casserole staple is cheese: plenty of it, and usually the nasty processed variety. Our recipes instead use small amounts of finely grated, lower-fat real cheese to make a sauce that's just as smooth. A sharper cheese will give you more flavor, as will the addition of herbs and spices.

3. Top It Off

A casserole's topping is typically made of gobs of cheese (yep, more cheese), with heavily buttered bread crumbs or biscuits, or those infamous canned fried onions. In other words, it's a horror show for the arteries. Update your topping by moistening bread crumbs with just a light amount of olive oil instead of the butter, plus a sprinkling of Parmesan or Romano.

A biscuit topping can be made lighter in fat and calories, too. In the **Biscuit and Hamburger Pie**, for example, we used low-fat buttermilk to make it fluffy, substituted olive oil for butter, and added in whole wheat flour.

HOW TO GRILL LIKE A PRO

Is there anything that says "summer's here!" more than a great cookout? And is there anything more disappointing than dried-out grilled chicken, raw-in-the-middle burgers, and burned kebabs? That said, once you learn how to do it, cooking on the grill can be one of the healthiest and tastiest ways to prepare food. We've stripped grilling down to its basics, giving you all the tools you need to make a great meal—"Kiss the Cook" apron not included.

1. Choose Your Tools

The first question any aspiring griller must tackle: charcoal or gas? Each has its advantages. Charcoal grills are thought to give food more of a smoky flavor (as do any flavored wood chips you add). They're also generally cheaper than gas grills. But they are messier and take more work. Gas grills need less supervision and they're more predictable—you can control the heat with a turn of the dial.

Depending on what you're planning to cook, you'll also want to gather some or all of the following:

- **A pair of long-handled tongs** for moving food around on the grill (the giant fork that comes with most barbecue sets is useless; it will pierce meats and let all the juices run out).
- **A large spatula** for flipping burgers or turning whole fish.
- **Elbow-length oven mitts**, hot pads, and dish towels.
- **A long-handled pastry brush** for applying sauces and glazes.
- **Skewers.** Wood ones are better than metal, as they don't poke large holes in the food. Use two at once, and you'll keep food items from spinning around on the grill.
- **A side table** to hold plates, food, etc.
- **Clean plates and platters** for food coming off the grill (don't put cooked foods on dishes that have already held raw meat).
- **Heavy-duty aluminum foil** to package up delicate vegetables, and for whole fish. Alternatively, you can use vegetable or fish baskets, but choose nonstick or be sure to coat them well with cooking spray.
- **An instant-read thermometer** to check on foods that grill slowly.

2. Do Your Prep Work

Preparation is key no matter how you're cooking, but when you're working on the grill, it's particularly crucial. If you gather all your supplies and do all the food prep in advance, you won't have to leave the grill unattended while you run inside. You'll need to remember to marinate if necessary and, if you're using wood skewers for kebabs, soak the skewers in water for at least 30 minutes before loading them up with meat or veggies. That way they're less likely to burn.

Always make sure your grill grate is clean before you start cooking. For best results, scrub a metal grate with a wire brush (or a big wad of crumpled tinfoil) after it begins to warm up. Finally, even if your guests are starting to grumble, wait until your grill is thoroughly heated before beginning to cook.

3. Get Grilling

The two main methods of grilling are known as direct heat and indirect heat. In direct grilling, the food sits right over the heat source. This is best for vegetables, lean fish, and small pieces of poultry. In indirect grilling, the food sits on the cooler side of the grill, farthest from the hot coals or the flame (for charcoal, you'll want to load the coals in advance so that one side will be fuller than the other). But even foods that are typically grilled on direct heat can benefit from resting on a cooler part of the grill to finish off so they stay juicy. The best foods to grill indirectly are tougher cuts of meat, large roasts, and whole chickens and turkeys.

TECHNIQUE: LIGHTING UP

Natural hardwood charcoal burns cleaner and hotter than briquettes, which often contain fillers. If you do use briquettes, choose those labeled hardwood and avoid the self-lighting kind, which are saturated with petroleum.

You can use starter fluid if you like, but it's easy to light a charcoal fire with a chimney starter: Load the top of the metal canister with charcoal, stuff newspaper in the bottom, and light the paper with a match. The updraft spreads the fire from the paper to the charcoal and in 30 minutes your coals will glow. Turn the starter over to dump out the coals. Spread them evenly or, if you are going to do indirect grilling, bank the coals to one side of the grill.

And remember, don't use gasoline or highly volatile fluids to ignite charcoal. And never add starter fluid to an existing fire.

How you work once you're cooking is also important. Don't place food too close together on the grill; air needs to circulate around the food so that it sears properly, and your fire also has to have the air it needs for fuel. And don't move the food around too often. You won't have sticking problems if you let the food really sear and turn it only once. There are several recipes throughout this book that are terrific on the grill. Use the new tips you've learned to make all your grilled meals perfect!

BREAKFAST

ONION, SHALLOT, AND HERB FRITTATA

2 teaspoons olive oil, divided

1 cup chopped onion

2 tablespoons minced shallot

2 eggs

4 egg whites

1/4 cup minced fresh basil

Salt and pepper to taste

2 tablespoons freshly grated Parmesan or Romano cheese

1 Preheat the oven to 350°F. Heat 1 teaspoon of the olive oil in a large nonstick ovenproof skillet over medium heat. Add the onion and shallot and sauté for about 7 to 8 minutes. Remove the onion mixture from the skillet and set aside.

2 Beat the eggs, egg whites, basil, and salt and pepper. Fold in the onion mixture.

3 In the remaining 1 teaspoon of oil, heat the egg mixture on medium low. Cook without stirring for about 8 minutes.

4 Transfer the skillet to the oven, sprinkle with the cheese, and bake for about 10 minutes until top is no longer runny. Cook an additional 5 minutes if necessary. Cut into wedges to serve.

11

Calories 70	Total Fat 4 g	Cholesterol 70 mg	Total Carbohydrate 4 g	Protein 6 g
Calories from Fat 35	Saturated Fat 1.1 g	Sodium 75 mg*	Dietary Fiber 1 g	Phosphorus 60 mg
	Trans Fat 0 g	Potassium 120 mg	Sugars 2 g	

*without added salt

BREAKFAST

MEXICALI BREAKFAST EGGS ✓

4 small (6-inch) whole-wheat tortillas

2 teaspoons canola oil

1/2 cup diced onion

3 garlic cloves, minced

2 scallions, minced

1/2 cup sliced red pepper

1 tablespoon seeded and diced jalapeño pepper (optional, not included in nutritional analysis)

1/2 teaspoon cumin

7 egg whites

3 whole eggs

1/3 cup fat-free milk

1/4 teaspoon dried oregano
Salt and pepper to taste

GARNISH

1/2 cup hot or mild salsa

1/4 cup nonfat Greek yogurt (optional, not included in nutritional analysis)

1 Preheat the oven to 400°F. Wrap the tortillas in foil and place them on a baking sheet in the oven to warm while you prepare the eggs.

2 Heat the oil in a large nonstick skillet over medium heat. Add the onion and garlic and sauté for 3 minutes. Add in the scallions and red pepper and sauté for 3 minutes. Add in the jalapeno peppers and cumin and sauté for 1 minute.

3 Whip together the egg whites, eggs, milk, oregano, salt, and pepper. Pour over the vegetable mixture and lightly scramble the eggs until desired doneness.

4 To serve, divide the egg mixture among the hot tortillas and roll into cones. Serve with the salsa and a dollop of Greek yogurt if desired.

13

Calories 225	Total Fat 7 g	Cholesterol 160 mg	Total Carbohydrate 24 g	Protein 15 g
Calories from Fat 65	Saturated Fat 1.7 g	Sodium 565 mg*	Dietary Fiber 3 g	Phosphorus 165 mg
	Trans Fat 0 g	Potassium 410 mg	Sugars 6 g	

*without added salt

BREAKFAST

CARROT APRICOT POWER MUFFINS

1/4 cup raw, unsalted sunflower seeds

2 tablespoons sesame seeds

1 3/4 cups all-purpose flour

2 teaspoons baking powder

1/2 teaspoon baking soda

1 teaspoon cinnamon

3/4 teaspoon ground ginger

1 cup low-fat buttermilk

1/4 cup light olive oil

1/2 cup Splenda brown sugar blend

1 large egg

3 large carrots, peeled and shredded

1/3 cup dried apricots, finely chopped

1 Preheat the oven to 375°F. Coat a nonstick 12-cup muffin tin with cooking spray.

2 Spread the sunflower seeds and sesame seeds onto a baking sheet. Bake the seeds for about 3 to 4 minutes until lightly toasted. Remove from the oven. Keep the oven on.

3 In a large bowl, combine the flour, baking powder, baking soda, cinnamon, and ginger.

4 In a separate bowl, whisk together the buttermilk, oil, Splenda, and egg until well combined. Make a well in the center of the dry ingredients and add the egg mixture. Stir until just combined.

5 Fold in the sunflower and sesame seeds, shredded carrots, and apricots.

6 Spoon the batter into the prepared muffin tin and bake for about 25 to 30 minutes until a toothpick inserted into the center comes out clean. Let the muffins cool 5 minutes in the pan and then turn them out onto a cooling rack.

Calories 200	Total Fat 8 g	Cholesterol 20 mg	Total Carbohydrate 29 g	Protein 4 g
Calories from Fat 70	Saturated Fat 1.1 g	Sodium 155 mg	Dietary Fiber 2 g	Phosphorus 160 mg
	Trans Fat 0 g	Potassium 200 mg	Sugars 12 g	

SPRING LEEK FRITTATA

2 1/2 teaspoons olive oil

2 medium leeks, bottom part only, washed and thinly sliced

2 garlic cloves, minced

1/2 cup reduced-sodium ham, diced

2 eggs

5 egg whites

1/4 cup fat-free milk

1 teaspoon dried basil

1/2 teaspoon dried thyme

Salt and pepper to taste

2 tablespoons shredded reduced-fat Swiss cheese

1 In a 10-inch nonstick oven-proof skillet or cast-iron skillet, heat the oil over medium heat. Add the leeks and garlic, and sauté for about 8 to 9 minutes until leeks are very soft. Add the ham and sauté for 2 minutes.

2 In a bowl, beat together the eggs, egg whites, milk, basil, thyme, and salt and pepper to taste.

3 Preheat the oven broiler, with the rack set 6 inches from the heat source. Slowly add the egg mixture on top of the leeks. Cook undisturbed for about 3 minutes. Using a thin-bladed spatula, lift up some of the eggs from the sides and tilt the pan to allow some of the eggs on top to fall to the bottom of the pan. Continue to cook the frittata until the frittata is no longer runny, but the top has some uncooked egg.

4 Top the frittata with the Swiss cheese. Place the frittata in the oven and broil until the cheese melts and the top is set. Cut into wedges directly from the pan to serve.

17

Calories 95	Total Fat 4.5 g	Cholesterol 75 mg	Total Carbohydrate 6 g	Protein 9 g
Calories from Fat 40	Saturated Fat 1.1 g	Sodium 180 mg*	Dietary Fiber 1 g	Phosphorus 95 mg
	Trans Fat 0 g	Potassium 170 mg	Sugars 2 g	

*without added salt

BREAKFAST

APPLE CINNAMON COUSCOUS BREAKFAST

1 1/2 cups fat-free milk

1 tablespoon agave nectar

1 1/2 teaspoons cinnamon

1 cup couscous

1 small apple with peel, grated

1/4 cup roughly chopped dried cherries

1/4 cup unsweetened apple juice

2 tablespoons toasted chopped walnuts

1 In a saucepan, bring the milk, agave nectar, and cinnamon to a boil. Add the couscous, cover, and turn off the heat. Let the couscous rest and absorb the milk.

2 When the couscous has absorbed the milk, add the grated apple, dried cherries, apple juice, and walnuts.

Calories 145	Total Fat 1.5 g	Cholesterol 0 mg	Total Carbohydrate 28 g	Protein 5 g
Calories from Fat 15	Saturated Fat 0.1 g	Sodium 30 mg	Dietary Fiber 2 g	Phosphorus 120 mg
	Trans Fat 0 g	Potassium 155 mg	Sugars 10 g	

BREAKFAST

BROCCOLI AND SWISS SOUFFLÉ

2 teaspoons olive oil

1/2 cup chopped onion

3 tablespoons minced scallions

Salt and pepper to taste

2 tablespoons all-purpose flour

1 cup 1% milk

1 egg yolk, beaten

1/2 cup shredded, reduced-fat Swiss cheese

1 (10-ounce) package frozen chopped broccoli, thawed, drained, and patted dry

6 egg whites, lightly beaten

1/4 teaspoon cream of tartar

1 Preheat the oven to 400°F. Coat a 1½-quart soufflé dish with cooking spray, and set aside.

2 Heat the olive oil in a large skillet over medium heat. Add the onions and scallions, and sauté for 5 minutes. Remove the skillet from the heat. Add in the salt, pepper, and flour and mix well. Gradually add half the milk, stirring constantly with a wire whisk. Add in the remaining milk, and return the pan to the stove. Whisk constantly for 2 minutes until sauce is thick. Remove the pan from the heat.

3 Add the egg yolk to a bowl. Pour in the milk mixture, and whisk until smooth. Add the mixture back to the same skillet, and cook for 1 minute. Add in the Swiss cheese and thawed broccoli. Set aside.

4 Beat the egg whites with the cream of tartar on high speed with an electric mixer until stiff. Add a small amount of the egg yolk mixture to the egg whites and fold in gently. Add the remaining egg yolk mixture to the egg whites, folding carefully until the egg white is fully incorporated. Spoon the mixture into the soufflé dish. Bake for 30 minutes until the soufflé is set. Serve immediately.

21

Calories 85	Total Fat 3.5 g	Cholesterol 30 mg	Total Carbohydrate 6 g	Protein 8 g
Calories from Fat 30	Saturated Fat 1.3 g	Sodium 75 mg*	Dietary Fiber 1 g	Phosphorus 105 mg
	Trans Fat 0 g	Potassium 190 mg	Sugars 3 g	

*without added salt

CHEESE AND SPINACH PUFF

Cooking spray

3 cups 1% milk

1/2 cup diced onions

3/4 cup yellow cornmeal

2 large egg yolks

1 package (10 ounce) frozen chopped spinach, thawed, drained, and patted dry

3/4 cup extra-sharp, reduced-fat cheddar cheese, finely shredded, not packed

1/2 teaspoon salt

Fresh-ground black pepper

7 large egg whites

1 Preheat the oven to 375°F. Coat a 9×13–inch baking pan with cooking spray.

2 In a large saucepot, bring the milk and onions to a simmer over medium heat. Add the cornmeal, whisking constantly, until the mixture has thickened. Remove from the heat. Add in the egg yolks, spinach, cheese, salt, and pepper.

3 Beat the egg whites with an electric mixer until soft peaks form. Slowly add the whites to the egg yolk, spinach, and cornmeal mixture, folding gently.

4 Pour the mixture into the pan, and bake for 30 to 35 minutes until golden brown and puffed. (This will puff up but deflate quickly.) Serve immediately.

23

Calories 155	Total Fat 4.5 g	Cholesterol 60 mg	Total Carbohydrate 18 g	Protein 12 g
Calories from Fat 40	Saturated Fat 2.4 g	Sodium 350 mg	Dietary Fiber 2 g	Phosphorus 200 mg
	Trans Fat 0 g	Potassium 315 mg	Sugars 6 g	

SPINACH AND MUSHROOM FRITTATA

1 1/2 teaspoons olive oil

1/4 cup coarsely chopped fresh mushrooms

1/4 cup baby spinach leaves, stems removed

1 whole egg

3 egg whites

Kosher salt and freshly ground black pepper to taste

1 tablespoon fat-free feta cheese

1 Preheat the oven broiler. Heat the oil in a 7-inch heatproof skillet, on medium-high heat. Add the mushrooms, and sauté for 3 minutes. Add the spinach, and cook just until the spinach wilts, about 30 seconds. Pour off any accumulated liquid.

2 Beat the egg and egg whites with salt and pepper in a small bowl. Pour the mixture over the mushrooms and spinach. Let the eggs set over medium-high heat, repeatedly lifting the edges to allow uncooked egg to flow to the bottom, about 3 to 5 minutes. When the frittata is almost set, sprinkle with feta cheese.

3 Set the pan under the oven broiler, about 6 inches from the heat source. Broil until the top is set and the cheese is melted, 3 to 5 minutes.

Calories 195	Total Fat 12 g	Cholesterol 210 mg	Total Carbohydrate 3 g	Protein 20 g
Calories from Fat 110	Saturated Fat 2.5 g	Sodium 385 mg*	Dietary Fiber 0 g	Phosphorus 165 mg
	Trans Fat 0 g	Potassium 370 mg	Sugars 2 g	

*without added salt

BREAKFAST

TWO GREENS FRITTATA

1 tablespoon olive oil, divided

2 large garlic cloves, minced

8 cups stemmed, bite-size pieces of mixed fresh Swiss chard and fresh spinach*

2 eggs

4 egg whites

1/4 cup low-fat (1%) cottage cheese

1 teaspoon dried oregano

1/2 teaspoon dried thyme leaves

Pinch crushed red pepper flakes

Ground black pepper to taste

After cleaning the greens, leave a little moisture clinging to the leaves.

1 Heat 2 teaspoons of the oil in a large ovenproof skillet over medium heat. Add the minced garlic and sauté for 30 seconds. Add the greens. Using tongs, turn the greens and cook for about 7 minutes, making sure not to burn the garlic, until the leaves are wilted and tender. Drain any excess liquid and turn the greens onto a plate or bowl; set aside. Wipe the skillet clean.

2 Preheat an oven broiler with the rack set 6 inches from the heat source. Combine the eggs, egg whites, cottage cheese, oregano, thyme, and red pepper flakes in a food processor or blender. Process for 30 seconds.

3 Heat the remaining 1 teaspoon of oil in the skillet on medium heat. Add the greens, spreading them evenly over the pan. Pour the egg mixture on top of the greens and cook, undisturbed, for 3 to 4 minutes. With a spatula, lift the edges of the eggs so the uncooked eggs can flow to the bottom of the pan to cook.

4 Once the eggs are almost set but the center is a bit runny, place the pan under the broiler and broil for 1 to 2 minutes until the eggs are set and the top is golden. Cut into wedges and sprinkle with black pepper to serve.

COOK'S TIP | Greens such as spinach shrink considerably when cooked. Plan on 3 ounces of raw spinach leaves to serve each person.

Calories 110	Total Fat 6 g	Cholesterol 95 mg	Total Carbohydrate 4 g	Protein 10 g
Calories from Fat 55	Saturated Fat 1.4 g	Sodium 250 mg	Dietary Fiber 1g	Phosphorus 110 mg
	Trans Fat 0 g	Potassium 415 mg	Sugars 1g	

STARTERS

SPICY FINGER LICKIN' FRIED CHICKEN STRIPS WITH BLUE CHEESE DRESSING

CHICKEN

- 1 pound chicken tenders
- 1/2 cup low-fat buttermilk
  Several drops hot sauce
- 1/2 cup flour
- 1/2 teaspoon paprika
- 1/2 teaspoon black pepper
- 1/4 teaspoon ground red pepper
- 1 1/2 tablespoons canola oil

DRESSING

- 1/2 cup nonfat mayonnaise
- 1 tablespoon red wine vinegar
- 1 teaspoon bottled minced garlic
- 1 1/3 tablespoons crumbled blue cheese
- 1/4 teaspoon black pepper

1 Coat each tender in a mixture of the buttermilk and hot sauce.

2 Combine the flour, paprika, black pepper, and ground red pepper. Dredge each tender in the flour mixture, shaking off excess.

3 Heat the oil in a large nonstick skillet over medium-high heat. Add the tenders and cook for about 3 minutes per side. Remove and drain on paper towels.

4 Combine all the dressing ingredients. Serve the chicken with some of the dressing on the side.

Calories 175	Total Fat 6 g	Cholesterol 45 mg	Total Carbohydrate 10 g	Protein 18 g
Calories from Fat 55	Saturated Fat 1.2 g	Sodium 220 mg	Dietary Fiber 0 g	Phosphorus 155 mg
	Trans Fat 0 g	Potassium 190 mg	Sugars 2 g	

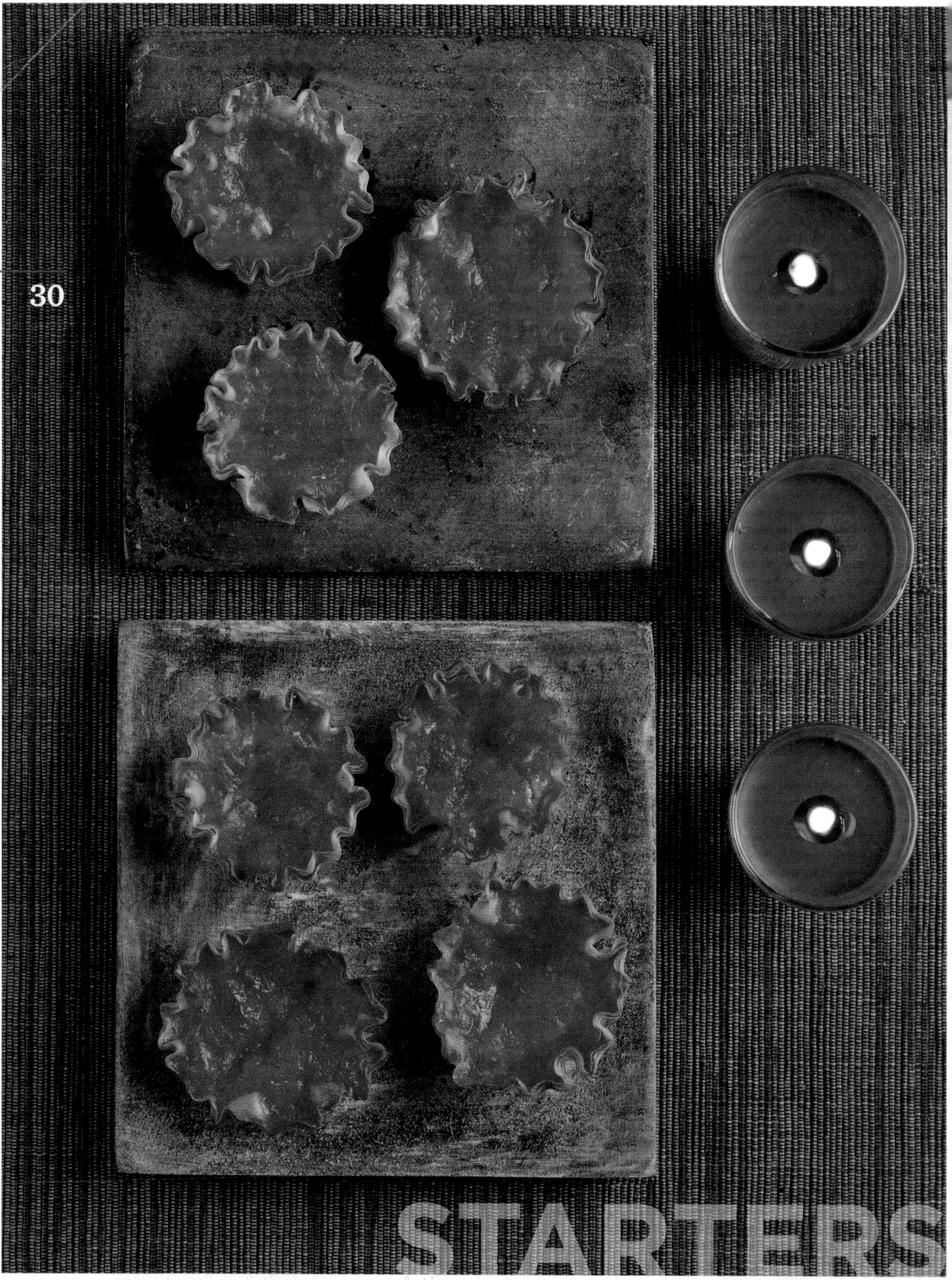

STARTERS

MINI CHEESE QUICHES

24 frozen phyllo dough mini shells

2 eggs, beaten

1/2 cup fat-free milk

1 tablespoon melted butter

1/2 teaspoon salt

1 cup shredded 75% reduced-fat cheddar cheese (extra sharp if available)

Paprika (not included in nutritional analysis)

1 Preheat the oven to 350°F. Place the shells on a baking sheet, and bake for 5 minutes.

2 Beat together the eggs, milk, butter, and salt. Once the shells are ready, distribute the cheese into each shell. Pour the egg mixture into each shell. Sprinkle with paprika. Bake for 25 minutes or until set.

31

Calories 80
Calories from Fat 40

Total Fat 4.5 g
Saturated Fat 1.4 g
Trans Fat 0 g

Cholesterol 40 mg
Sodium 210 mg
Potassium 45 mg

Total Carbohydrate 5 g
Dietary Fiber 0 g
Sugars 1 g

Protein 4 g
Phosphorus 80 mg

32

YOGURT DIP WITH ZAHTAR PITAS

ZAHTAR

1/2 cup sesame seeds

2 tablespoons ground sumac

2 tablespoons ground dried thyme

YOGURT

2 cups nonfat Greek-style yogurt

3 teaspoons olive oil, divided

Fresh ground black pepper

1 garlic clove, minced

1/2 teaspoon lemon zest

BREAD

3 small whole-wheat pitas (about 1 ounce each)

1 Preheat the oven to 350°F. To prepare the zahtar, toast the sesame seeds in a dry skillet over medium heat until seeds are lightly browned. Add in the sumac and dried thyme. Set aside.

2 For the dip, mix together the yogurt and 1 teaspoon of the olive oil. Add about 2 tablespoons of the zahtar, fresh ground black pepper to taste, the minced garlic, and lemon zest.

3 Brush the remaining olive oil over the pitas. Sprinkle with about 1 teaspoon of zahtar per pita. Store the remaining zahtar in an airtight container. Cut the pitas into wedges, and place them on a baking sheet. Bake for about 12 to 15 minutes until crisp. Add a bowl of yogurt dip in the middle of a platter. Surround with the zahtar pita pieces.

Calories 120	**Total Fat 4 g**	**Cholesterol 0 mg**	**Total Carbohydrate 12 g**	**Protein 9 g**
Calories from Fat 35	Saturated Fat 0.6 g	**Sodium 105 mg**	Dietary Fiber 2 g	**Phosphorus 175 mg**
	Trans Fat 0 g	**Potassium 250 mg**	Sugars 3 g	

CLASSIC BAKED ARTICHOKE DIP

1/2 cup reduced-fat mayonnaise

1/4 cup grated fresh Parmesan cheese

1/4 cup finely chopped celery

1/4 cup finely chopped onion

2 tablespoons minced parsley

1 teaspoon garlic powder

1/2 teaspoon fresh-ground black pepper

1/2 teaspoon salt

Pinch ground red pepper (not included in nutritional analysis)

1 (14-ounce) can artichoke hearts, drained and chopped

12 ounces fat-free cream cheese

4 ounces reduced-fat cream cheese

1 Preheat the oven to 350°F. Coat a 2-quart casserole dish with cooking spray. In a large bowl, combine all the ingredients, and stir until well blended.

2 Spoon the mixture into the prepared dish, and bake for 30 minutes.

Calories 45	Total Fat 2.5 g	Cholesterol 5 mg	Total Carbohydrate 2 g	Protein 2 g
Calories from Fat 20	Saturated Fat 0.9 g	Sodium 215 mg	Dietary Fiber 0 g	Phosphorus 80 mg
	Trans Fat 0 g	Potassium 70 mg	Sugars 1 g	

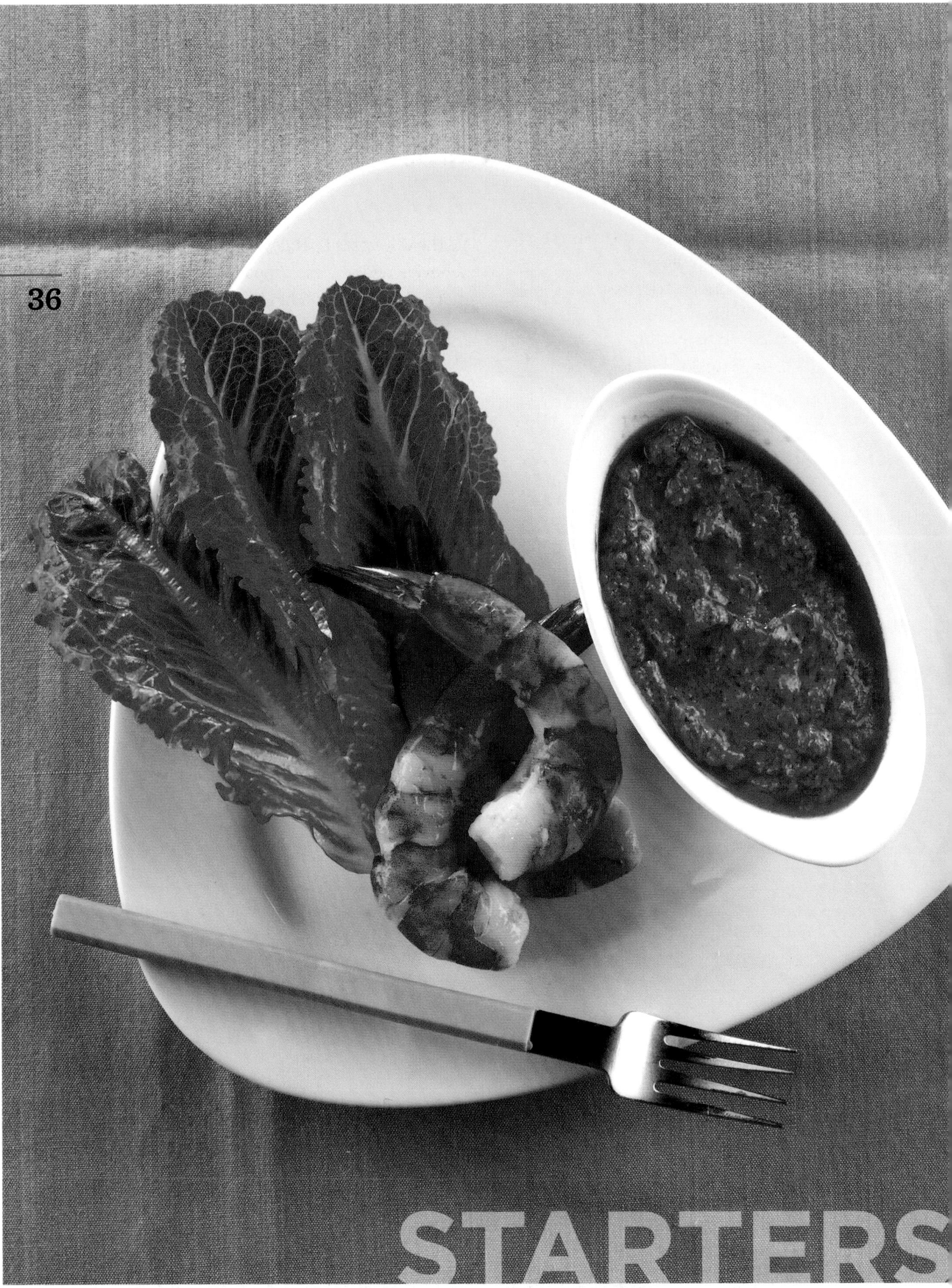

STARTERS

AVOCADO HERB DRESSING

2 cups watercress leaves, stems removed

1/4 cup chopped fresh parsley

1/4 cup minced fresh chives

2 tablespoons minced fresh tarragon

2 anchovy filets, drained of any oil

1 garlic clove, chopped

1 cup extra-virgin olive oil, divided

1/2 small ripe avocado, cubed

Juice of 1 1/2 medium lemons

Sea salt and freshly ground black pepper to taste

1 Add the watercress, parsley, chives, tarragon, anchovies, and garlic to a food processor, and process for 1 minute. Add 1/2 cup of the olive oil, and blend until smooth. Remove the herb mixture from the food processor, and add it to a bowl. Clean out the food processor "work bowl."

2 Add the avocado and lemon juice to the food processor bowl, and process until smooth. In a thin stream, slowly add the remaining olive oil. Add in the reserved herb mixture, season with salt and pepper, and process for 1 minute.

37

COOK'S TIP | Dressing can be stored in a sealed container for up to 4 days in the refrigerator.

Calories 70	Total Fat 7 g	Cholesterol 0 mg	Total Carbohydrate 0 g	Protein 0 g
Calories from Fat 65	Saturated Fat 1 g	Sodium 10 mg*	Dietary Fiber 0 g	Phosphorus 5 mg
	Trans Fat 0 g	Potassium 29 mg	Sugars 0 g	
				*without added salt

STARTERS

SPICY PROSCIUTTO SHRIMP

MARINADE

- 1/4 cup fresh lemon juice
- 1/4 cup reduced-sodium soy sauce
- 3 tablespoons rice wine (mirin)
- 1 tablespoon grated fresh ginger
- 3 scallions, minced
- 1 1/2 teaspoons toasted sesame oil

- 32 medium shrimp, peeled and deveined
- 16 wooden skewers
- 2 ounces prosciutto, cut into 32 thin strips

1 In a bowl, combine the marinade ingredients, and add the shrimp. Cover and marinate in the refrigerator for 1 to 2 hours.

2 Put the wooden skewers in a pan of warm water, and soak for an hour.

3 Preheat the oven broiler. Prepare a broiler tray lined with foil. Coat the foil with cooking spray.

4 Drain the shrimp from the marinade, and discard the marinade. Wrap a slice of prosciutto around each shrimp. Thread 4 shrimp onto a pair of skewers to keep the shrimp stabilized as they cook. Broil for 1 to 2 minutes per side. Serve hot or at room temperature.

Calories 45	Total Fat 1 g	Cholesterol 40 mg	Total Carbohydrate 1 g	Protein 7 g
Calories from Fat 10	Saturated Fat 0.3 g	Sodium 387 mg	Dietary Fiber 0 g	Phosphorus 70 mg
	Trans Fat 0 g	Potassium 85 mg	Sugars 0 g	

STARTERS

PAPAYA BRUSCHETTA

16 (1/2-inch-thick) slices French or Italian bread (about 1/2 ounce per slice)

2 garlic cloves, crushed

PAPAYA TOPPING

1/2 ripe medium papaya, seeded and diced

3 large plum tomatoes, seeded and diced

1/2 cup minced red onion

1/2 cup minced red bell pepper

2 tablespoons minced fresh basil

1 tablespoon minced scallion

1 tablespoon red wine vinegar

1 teaspoon sugar

Salt and freshly ground black pepper, optional

1 Preheat the oven to 400°F.

2 For the Papaya Topping: In a bowl, combine all ingredients for Papaya Topping and, if desired, salt and black pepper.

3 Place the bread slices on a large baking sheet. Toast the bread lightly for 3 to 4 minutes (the slices should still appear white).

4 Remove the bread from the oven, and immediately rub the top side of each slice with garlic. Spoon 2 tablespoons Papaya Topping on each bread slice. Serve immediately.

COOK'S TIP | Try the Papaya Topping as a free-food condiment for bruschetta, broiled seafood, grilled chicken, and fish tacos. To store: refrigerate covered; use within three days.

BRUSCHETTA WITH PAPAYA TOPPING

Calories 100	**Total Fat** 0.5 g	**Cholesterol** 0 mg	**Total Carbohydrate** 20 g	**Protein** 4 g
Calories from Fat 5	Saturated Fat 0.2 g	**Sodium** 195 mg*	Dietary Fiber 1 g	**Phosphorus** 45 mg
	Trans Fat 0 g	**Potassium** 135 mg	Sugars 3 g	

PAPAYA TOPPING ONLY

Calories 5	**Total Fat** 0 g	**Cholesterol** 0 mg	**Total Carbohydrate** 2 g	**Protein** 0 g
Calories from Fat 0	Saturated Fat 0 g	**Sodium** 0 mg*	Dietary Fiber 0 g	**Phosphorus** 0 mg
	Trans Fat 0 g	**Potassium** 45 mg	Sugars 1 g	

*without added salt

STARTERS

DIJON AND HORSERADISH DEVILED EGGS

6 large eggs

1 tablespoon white vinegar

6 tablespoons plain nonfat yogurt

1 tablespoon fat-free mayonnaise

1 tablespoon freshly minced chives

2 teaspoons Dijon mustard

1/2 teaspoon grated prepared horseradish

1/4 teaspoon turmeric

Sea salt and freshly ground black pepper to taste

GARNISH

Regular or smoked paprika

1 To prepare the eggs: Add the eggs to a saucepan that is large enough so they are not crowded. Add water to cover about 1 inch over the eggs. Cover the pot and bring to a boil. Once the water comes to a boil, about 6 to 7 minutes, remove the pot from the heat and set it on an unused burner. Add the vinegar to the water (to help in peeling the eggs). Let the eggs stand in the hot water for 20 to 30 minutes.

2 Prepare a large bowl of ice water. Using a slotted spoon, transfer the eggs to the ice water bath, letting them cool for 15 to 20 minutes. Gently remove each egg from the ice water, and gently tap its shell until it is cracked all over (but do not peel). Add the cracked eggs back to the ice water bath (prepare a new ice bath if necessary) for 10 minutes. Remove the eggs from the ice water, and gently roll them between your palms. The shells should slip off easily. Discard the shells.

3 Halve each egg and remove the yolks. Discard one yolk and add the remaining five to a bowl. Set the egg whites on a platter, with the cut sides up. Mash the yolks with the yogurt, mayonnaise, chives, mustard, horseradish, turmeric, salt, and pepper. Spoon or pipe the egg yolk mixture back into the egg whites. Sprinkle lightly with paprika.

COOK'S TIP | Boil week-old eggs; they are easier to peel. To help center the yolks of the eggs you plan to hard-boil, store the eggs on their side overnight in the refrigerator instead of upright.

Calories 75	Total Fat 4 g	Cholesterol 150 mg	Total Carbohydrate 3 g	Protein 7 g
Calories from Fat 35	Saturated Fat 1.4 g	Sodium 135 mg	Dietary Fiber 0 g	Phosphorus 85 mg
	Trans Fat 0 g	Potassium 110 mg	Sugars 2 g	

SPICY PEANUT SAUCE

1 cup reduced-fat creamy peanut butter

1 1/2 cups reduced-sodium, low-fat chicken broth

1/2 cup fresh lime juice

3 tablespoons brown sugar or 1 1/2 tablespoons Splenda Brown Sugar Blend

2 tablespoons light (lower-sodium) soy sauce

2 tablespoons peeled and grated fresh ginger

1/2 teaspoon crushed red chili flakes

1 Heat the peanut butter in a small saucepan over medium heat. Add the chicken broth, and mix until combined.

2 Add in the remaining ingredients, and cook over medium-low heat for 5 minutes, or until thickened. Use as sauce over cooked shrimp, scallops, chicken, turkey, or beef.

COOK'S TIP | Sauce can be stored in a sealed container for 2 to 3 days in the refrigerator.

Calories 85	**Total Fat 5 g**	**Cholesterol 0 mg**	**Total Carbohydrate 7 g**	**Protein 4 g**
Calories from Fat 45	Saturated Fat 0.8 g	**Sodium 145 mg**	Dietary Fiber 1 g	**Phosphorus 55 mg**
	Trans Fat 0 g	**Potassium 115 mg**	Sugars 3 g	

GRILLED PORK AND CHEESE QUESADILLAS

46

Cooking spray

1 pound ground pork loin

2 teaspoons minced garlic
   Salt and pepper to taste

1/2 cup reduced-fat cheddar cheese

1/2 cup reduced-fat Monterey Jack cheese

4 scallions, thinly sliced

1 (4-ounce) can chopped green chilies, drained

8 (6-inch) corn or whole-wheat flour tortillas

GARNISHES

1/2 cup nonfat sour cream or nonfat Greek-style yogurt

1/2 cup prepared Roasted Pepper and Cherry Tomato Salsa (next page).

1 Spray a nonstick skillet with cooking spray. Cook the ground pork and garlic for about 5 to 7 minutes, until there are no traces of pink in the meat. Drain any excess fat; season with salt and pepper to taste.

2 Combine the pork with the cheeses, scallions, and green chilies. Spread the filling evenly over 4 tortillas. Top with remaining tortillas to form a quesadilla and press lightly together.

3 Heat a nonstick pan over medium heat. Lightly coat the pan with cooking spray. Place the quesadillas in a pan and cook for 2 minutes on each side until lightly toasted. Cut into wedges to serve. Serve with sour cream and salsa.

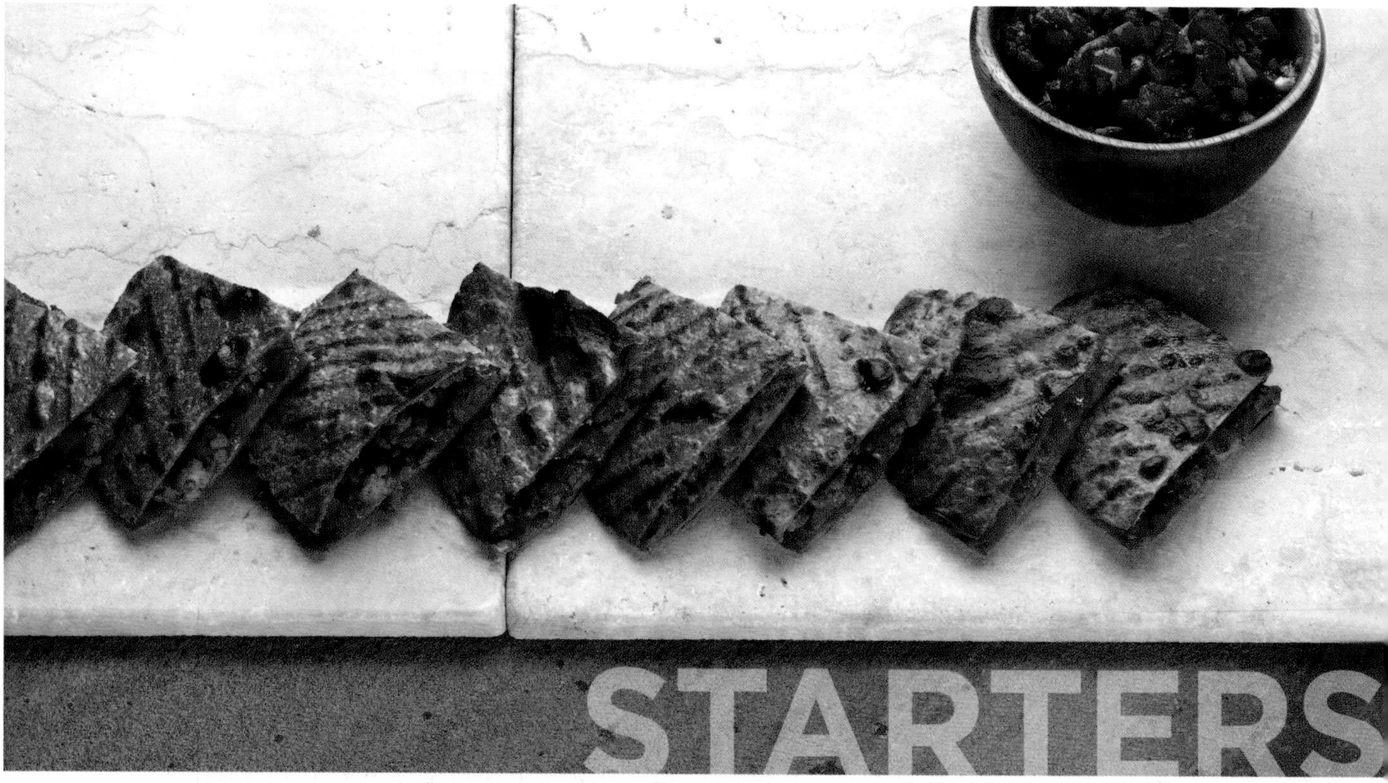

STARTERS

ROASTED PEPPER AND CHERRY TOMATO SALSA

2 medium red peppers

1 medium yellow pepper

1/2 cup diced cherry tomatoes

1/2 jalapeño pepper, seeded and minced

1/2 red onion, minced

2 garlic cloves, minced

2 tablespoons red wine vinegar or fresh lime juice

2 tablespoons minced cilantro

2 teaspoon olive oil

1 teaspoon chili powder

Salt and pepper to taste

1 Place the whole red and yellow peppers directly on an open stove flame. With long-handled tongs, keep turning the peppers until most of the skin has blackened. Place the peppers in a bowl and cover with plastic wrap. Set aside to cool.

Alternative method 1: Cut the peppers in half, and remove the seeds and white membrane. Place the peppers, skin side up, under an oven broiler, about 4 to 5 inches from the heat source. Broil the peppers until they are blackened. Place the peppers in a bowl, and cool as above.

Alternative method 2: Cook the whole peppers on an outdoor charcoal or gas grill. Place the peppers directly on a grill rack that has been coated with nonstick cooking spray. Set the heat to medium high. Cover the grill. Using long-handled tongs, keep checking the peppers by turning them to make sure all sides have blackened. Cool as above.

2 Once the peppers have cooled enough that they can be handled, remove them from the bowl. Peel off the charred skin with your fingers, using a paper towel for assistance. Don't worry about removing every bit of skin.

3 Discard the seeds and chop the peppers into a medium dice. Add them to a medium bowl. Add the remaining ingredients, cover, and let sit for about 1 hour.

47

COOK'S TIP | If using purchased salsa, sodium content will be much higher.

QUESADILLAS

Calories 85	**Total Fat 2.5 g**	**Cholesterol 20 mg**	**Total Carbohydrate 7 g**	**Protein 9 g**
Calories from Fat 20	Saturated Fat 1.2 g	**Sodium 95 mg***	Dietary Fiber 1 g	**Phosphorus 135 mg**
	Trans Fat 0 g	**Potassium 150 mg**	Sugars 1 g	

SALSA

Calories 10	**Total Fat 0 g**	**Cholesterol 0 mg**	**Total Carbohydrate 2 g**	**Protein 0 g**
Calories from Fat 0	Saturated Fat 0.1 g	**Sodium 0 mg***	Dietary Fiber 0 g	**Phosphorus 5 mg**
	Trans Fat 0 g	**Potassium 50 mg**	Sugars 1 g	

*without added salt

CHICKPEA TABBOULEH

1/2 cup fine bulgur wheat

    Hot water to cover and soak bulgur

2 bunches (about 1/2 pound) fresh parsley, thick stems removed

4 tablespoons minced fresh mint

1/2 cup peeled, seeded, and diced cucumber

3 scallions, finely minced (about 1/2 cup)

3 small tomatoes (about 1 pound), diced (about 2 1/2 cups)

1/2 medium red bell pepper, seeded and diced (about 1/2 cup)

1 cup canned chickpeas (garbanzos), drained and rinsed

VINAIGRETTE

3 tablespoons fresh lemon juice

3 tablespoons olive oil

1/4 teaspoon salt

1 Rinse the bulgur wheat and add it to a small bowl. Pour hot water over the bulgur to cover, and let soak for about 20 minutes, until doubled in size. Drain excess liquid, if any, and place the bulgur in a large bowl.

2 Chop the parsley to a medium-fine consistency. It should have some texture left in it and should not look pureed. Add the parsley to the bulgur wheat, and add all the remaining salad ingredients. Cover and set aside.

3 For the vinaigrette, in a small bowl, whisk together the ingredients. Add to the salad; taste and adjust any seasonings. Add more lemon juice if desired. Turn the tabbouleh out onto a platter to serve.

GREAT GRAIN | Fine-textured bulgur wheat is the authentic form of the grain for tabbouleh. Fine bulgur can be found at natural foods stores and specialty markets, and through mail order. Coarse bulgur may be substituted. The key to authentic tabbouleh is fresh parsley and mint; the bulgur plays a secondary role, hence the small quantity of it compared with the amount of herbs. Other herbs or greens may be substituted, such as basil or chopped arugula leaves.

Calories 95	Total Fat 4.5 g	Cholesterol 0 mg	Total Carbohydrate 12 g	Protein 3 g
Calories from Fat 40	Saturated Fat 0.6 g	**Sodium 110 mg**	Dietary Fiber 3 g	**Phosphorus 55 mg**
	Trans Fat 0 g	**Potassium 275 mg**	Sugars 3 g	

SALADS

WINTER SALAD WITH CITRUS

SALAD

  6 cups mixed greens

  1 cup grapefruit sections

  1 cup orange sections

  1 cup thinly sliced red onion

1/4 cup coarsely chopped toasted walnuts

DRESSING

  2 tablespoons raspberry vinegar

  1 tablespoon orange juice

  1 tablespoon balsamic vinegar

  1 tablespoon olive oil

1/2 teaspoon sugar

1/4 teaspoon pepper

1/2 teaspoon soy sauce

1/4 teaspoon dry mustard

1/8 teaspoon salt

1 Combine the dressing ingredients in a bowl.

2 Combine the greens, grapefruit, oranges, onion, and walnuts. Add dressing and toss to coat.

51

Calories 80	Total Fat 4.5 g	Cholesterol 0 mg	Total Carbohydrate 10 g	Protein 2 g
Calories from Fat 40	Saturated Fat 0.5 g	Sodium 65 mg	Dietary Fiber 2 g	Phosphorus 35 mg
	Trans Fat 0 g	Potassium 235 mg	Sugars 6 g	

ARUGULA AND ROASTED BEET SALAD WITH CHÈVRE CHEESE DRESSING

3 small beets, stems removed and bottoms trimmed

DRESSING

2 tablespoons white wine or champagne vinegar, or lemon juice for more of a citrus flavor

1/2 teaspoon Dijon mustard

1/2 teaspoon sugar

1 garlic clove, minced

1 tablespoon chèvre goat cheese

2 tablespoons olive oil

Salt and pepper to taste

SALAD

6 cups washed baby arugula

1 cup peeled, shredded carrots

1 Preheat the oven to 425°F. Wrap each beet in foil and place on a baking sheet. Roast the beets for 45 minutes to 1 hour until they are tender when pierced with a fork. Unwrap the beets and let cool.

2 Meanwhile, prepare the dressing: In a small bowl or measuring cup, combine the vinegar, mustard, sugar, and garlic. Whisk well. Add the cheese and whisk again. Slowly stream in the oil, whisking constantly, until the dressing is well mixed. Season with salt and pepper to taste.

3 Under running water, peel the beets by hand. Pat dry. Cut each beet into 6 wedges.

4 To assemble the salad: Divide the arugula among 6 salad plates. Top with carrots. Surround with 3 wedges of beets. Drizzle with the dressing.

53

Calories 75	Total Fat 5 g	Cholesterol 0 mg	Total Carbohydrate 6 g	Protein 2 g
Calories from Fat 45	Saturated Fat 1 g	Sodium 55 mg*	Dietary Fiber 1 g	Phosphorus 35 mg
	Trans Fat 0 g	Potassium 215 mg	Sugars 3 g	

*without added salt

SALADS

SUMMER FENNEL AND TOMATO SALAD

VINAIGRETTE

- 2 tablespoons white wine vinegar
- 2 teaspoons Dijon mustard
- 1 garlic clove, finely minced
- 1 teaspoon fennel seed, ground (place fennel seeds in a coffee or spice grinder)
- 2 tablespoons olive oil

SALAD

- 2 large red or yellow tomatoes, sliced in half and cut into thin wedges
- 2 medium fennel bulbs, trimmed and julienned, sliced into 1/4-inch pieces
- 1/4 cup thinly sliced red onion
- 4 cups mixed greens

1 In a small bowl, whisk together the vinegar, mustard, garlic, and fennel seed. Slowly whisk in the oil until the dressing is completely mixed together.

2 In a salad bowl, combine the tomatoes, fennel, and onions with the greens. Add the dressing, and toss lightly to coat with the vinaigrette.

Calories 120	Total Fat 7 g	Cholesterol 0 mg	Total Carbohydrate 13 g	Protein 3 g
Calories from Fat 65	Saturated Fat 0.9 g	Sodium 115 mg	Dietary Fiber 4 g	Phosphorus 85 mg
	Trans Fat 0 g	Potassium 695 mg	Sugars 6 g	

SALADS

WHEAT BERRY AND CORN SALAD

SALAD

1 cup raw wheat berries

5 cups water, divided

2 cups corn kernels (either fresh cut from the cob or frozen and thawed)

1/2 cup finely chopped celery

1/2 cup dried cherries

1/4 cup minced red onion

DRESSING

1/4 cup raspberry vinegar

2 tablespoons olive oil

1 tablespoon lemon juice

1 teaspoon grated orange zest

Salt and fresh ground pepper to taste

1 Rinse the wheat berries in a fine sieve. Place them in a bowl, and cover them with 2 cups of the water. Place the bowl of wheat berries in the refrigerator, and soak them overnight.

2 Drain the wheat berries, and rinse them again. Bring the remaining 3 cups of water to a boil. Add the wheat berries, cover, and reduce the heat to low. Cook for 1 hour, until the wheat berries are tender.

3 Combine the wheat berries with the remaining ingredients for the salad.

4 Whisk together the dressing ingredients and pour over the salad. Cover and refrigerate 1 hour before serving.

Calories 145	Total Fat 3.5 g	Cholesterol 0 mg	Total Carbohydrate 27 g	Protein 4 g
Calories from Fat 30	Saturated Fat 0.5 g	**Sodium 10 mg***	Dietary Fiber 3 g	**Phosphorus 115 mg**
	Trans Fat 0 g	**Potassium 170 mg**	Sugars 8 g	

*without added salt

SALADS

ORANGE AND WALNUT SALAD

SALAD

8 cups mixed salad greens

2 large carrots, peeled and thinly sliced

1 small red onion, thinly sliced

2 large oranges, peeled and sectioned

VINAIGRETTE

2 tablespoons fresh orange juice

2 tablespoons fresh lemon juice

1 tablespoon honey

2 teaspoons Dijon mustard

1/4 cup walnut oil

Sea salt and fresh ground black pepper to taste

1/4 cup toasted walnut pieces

1 Place the greens on a platter. Top with the carrots, onion, and oranges.

2 For the vinaigrette, whisk together the orange and lemon juices, honey, and mustard. Slowly add the oil in a thin stream, whisking constantly.

3 Drizzle the vinaigrette over the salad. Salt and pepper to taste, and top with the walnuts.

59

Calories 135	Total Fat 9 g	Cholesterol 0 mg	Total Carbohydrate 13 g	Protein 2 g
Calories from Fat 80	Saturated Fat 0.9 g	Sodium 55 mg*	Dietary Fiber 3 g	Phosphorus 45 mg
	Trans Fat 0 g	Potassium 285 mg	Sugars 9 g	

*without added salt

TROPICAL FRUIT AND VEGETABLE SALAD WITH CHILI AND CILANTRO DRESSING

DRESSING

1 1/2 tablespoons olive oil

3 teaspoons lime juice

1 teaspoon honey

1/2 fresh red chili, seeded and minced

2 teaspoons minced cilantro

SALAD

1/4 medium red onion, halved and sliced

1/2 English cucumber, unpeeled and thinly sliced

2 kiwi fruits, peeled and sliced

1 large mango, sliced

1 Whisk together the dressing ingredients. Add the red onion to the dressing and marinate for 30 minutes.

2 Arrange the cucumber, kiwi, and mango in a shallow serving bowl. Arrange the marinated onions with all the dressing on top of the mango mixture.

Calories 135	Total Fat 6 g	Cholesterol 0 mg	Total Carbohydrate 23 g	Protein 1 g
Calories from Fat 55	Saturated Fat 0.8 g	Sodium 5 mg	Dietary Fiber 3 g	Phosphorus 40 mg
	Trans Fat 0 g	Potassium 335 mg	Sugars 17 g	

APPLE AND FENNEL SALAD WITH CRANBERRIES AND WALNUTS

SALAD

2 medium Braeburn apples, unpeeled (about 6 ounces each)

2 teaspoons fresh lemon juice

1 large fennel bulb

1/2 medium red onion, very thinly sliced

DRESSING

2 tablespoons cider vinegar

1 tablespoon fresh lemon juice

1 tablespoon honey

2 teaspoons coarse Dijon mustard

1 garlic clove, finely minced

1/3 cup walnut oil

Sea salt and freshly ground black pepper to taste

4 cups baby arugula, washed and dried

GARNISHES

1/4 cup dried cranberries

1/4 cup toasted walnut pieces*

1/4 cup crumbled gorgonzola cheese

To toast walnuts: Add the walnuts to a small, dry skillet. Toast them over medium heat for 3 to 4 minutes, just until fragrant. Make sure the nuts do not burn.

1 Core and quarter the apples. Slice the apples into thin pieces, and add to a bowl. Sprinkle with the 2 teaspoons lemon juice, and toss to coat. Set aside.

2 Prepare the fennel: Cut off the stalks and fronds (the leafy part) from the fennel bulb (Save the stalks to flavor a homemade soup if desired.) Chop 2 teaspoon of the fennel fronds, and reserve for the dressing. (The remaining fronds can be saved for a few days in an airtight container.) Trim the base of the fennel bulb. If the outer layer of the bulb appears to be dry and tough, remove it and discard. With a sharp knife, cut the remaining bulb into julienned pieces. Add the fennel to the apples. Add the red onion and toss.

3 Prepare the dressing: In a small bowl, whisk together the cider vinegar, lemon juice, honey, mustard, garlic, and the reserved 2 teaspoons of chopped fennel fronds. Slowly add the oil in a thin stream, whisking it in until the dressing is emulsified. Season the dressing with salt and pepper.

4 Add the arugula to a large bowl. Add in half of the dressing and toss well (using tongs helps distribute the dressing). Pile the arugula on a large platter. Add the remaining dressing to the apple-fennel mixture. Put the salad on top of the arugula.

5 Garnish the salad with the cranberries, walnuts, and cheese.

Calories 115	Total Fat 9 g	Cholesterol 0 mg	Total Carbohydrate 10 g	Protein 2 g
Calories from Fat 80	Saturated Fat 1.2 g	Sodium 70 mg	Dietary Fiber 2 g	Phosphorus 35 mg
	Trans Fat 0 g	Potassium 140 mg	Sugars 7 g	

SOUPS

CELERY ROOT AND POTATO SOUP

1 1/2 pounds celery root
(celeriac)

2 tablespoons olive oil

1 large onion, chopped

6 cups reduced-sodium,
low-fat chicken broth

1 1/2 pound Idaho potatoes,
peeled and quartered

Salt and pepper to taste

1 cup 1% milk

1 Trim the base of the celery root with a knife and then peel the skin with a vegetable peeler. Rinse the celery root and slice it into 1/4-inch slices.

2 Heat the oil in a large saucepan over medium heat, add the onion, and sauté for 5 minutes. Add the celery root and chicken broth. Bring to a boil, cover, and simmer for 5 minutes. Add in the potatoes and salt and pepper. Cover and simmer for 25 minutes until the vegetables are very soft.

3 Puree the vegetables with the liquid in batches in a food processor. Return to the saucepan and heat over medium heat. Gradually add the milk and heat, but do not boil. Readjust seasonings if necessary and serve.

Calories 95	Total Fat 2.5 g	Cholesterol 0 mg	Total Carbohydrate 15 g	Protein 3 g
Calories from Fat 20	Saturated Fat 0.4 g	Sodium 295 mg*	Dietary Fiber 2 g	Phosphorus 90 mg
	Trans Fat 0 g	Potassium 365 mg	Sugars 3 g	

*without added salt

SOUPS

ESCAROLE AND WHITE BEAN SOUP

2 teaspoons olive oil

1 medium onion, chopped

2 garlic cloves, minced

1 large carrot, peeled and diced

1 celery stalk, diced

1 tablespoon flour

4 cups low-fat, reduced-sodium chicken broth

1 (14 1/2-ounce) can diced tomatoes, undrained

1 (15-ounce) can cannellini or other white beans, drained and rinsed

1 teaspoon dried oregano

1/2 teaspoon dried rosemary

2 cups washed and chopped escarole

Salt and pepper to taste

1 In a large saucepot, heat the olive oil over medium-high heat. Add the onion, garlic, carrot, and celery and sauté for 6 minutes. Add in the flour and cook for 2 minutes. Add in the broth, tomatoes, beans, oregano, and rosemary and bring to a boil. Lower the heat and simmer, uncovered, for 20 minutes.

2 Add in the escarole and cook for 5 minutes, until the escarole wilts. Season with salt and pepper.

Calories 85	Total Fat 1.5 g	Cholesterol 0 mg	Total Carbohydrate 14 g	Protein 5 g
Calories from Fat 15	Saturated Fat 0.2 g	Sodium 395 mg*	Dietary Fiber 4 g	Phosphorus 85 mg
	Trans Fat 0 g	Potassium 420 mg	Sugars 3 g	

*without added salt

SOUPS

LEMONGRASS SHRIMP SOUP

6 cups low-fat, reduced-sodium chicken broth

3 stalks fresh lemongrass
Grated zest of 1 lime

2 tablespoons fresh lime juice

1 cup "lite" coconut milk

1 pound large shrimp, peeled and deveined

GARNISH

3 tablespoons minced cilantro

1 red chili, minced

1 Heat the chicken broth in a large saucepot over medium-high heat. Remove any outer dried leaves of each stalk of lemongrass. Cut 3 pieces from the bottom of each stalk into 2-inch lengths. Discard the upper two-thirds of each stalk.

2 Add the lemongrass pieces and lime zest to the chicken broth. Bring to a boil, lower the heat, and simmer for 10 minutes. Strain the broth, and return the broth to the saucepot. Add the lime juice and coconut milk. Add the shrimp, and simmer on medium heat for 4 minutes until shrimp is cooked through.

3 Garnish each bowl with some of the cilantro and red chili.

Calories 65	Total Fat 2 g	Cholesterol 65 mg	Total Carbohydrate 3 g	Protein 9 g
Calories from Fat 20	Saturated Fat 1.1 g	Sodium 695 mg	Dietary Fiber 0 g	Phosphorus 155 mg
	Trans Fat 0 g	Potassium 275 mg	Sugars 1 g	

SOUPS

ASIAN MUSHROOM SOUP

1 ounce dried shiitake mushrooms

5 cups low-fat, reduced-sodium vegetable stock, divided

2 teaspoons toasted sesame oil

2 small shallots, minced

2 garlic cloves, minced

1 large carrot, peeled and thinly sliced on a diagonal

1 celery stalk, thinly sliced on a diagonal

8 ounces sliced fresh cremini or button mushrooms

2 tablespoons light soy sauce

1 tablespoon rice vinegar

1/4 teaspoon hot sesame oil

3 scallions, minced

1 Add the dried shiitake mushrooms to a heatproof bowl. Heat 1 cup of the vegetable broth in a small saucepan over medium heat until just simmering, or in the microwave for 1 1/2 minutes on high.

2 Pour the hot stock over the dried mushrooms, and let stand at room temperature for about 15 minutes.

3 Heat the 2 teaspoons toasted sesame oil in a large saucepot over medium heat. Add the shallots, garlic, carrots, and celery, and sauté for 2 minutes. Cover and cook on medium-low heat for about 3 to 4 minutes.

4 Drain the shiitake mushrooms, discard the liquid, and slice the mushrooms into 1/4-inch pieces.

5 Uncover the pot, increase heat to medium, and add the fresh cremini or button mushrooms. Sauté for about 2 to 3 minutes until mushrooms are browned. Add in the sliced shiitake mushrooms. Add in the remaining 4 cups of vegetable broth, and simmer uncovered for 10 minutes.

6 Stir in the soy sauce, rice vinegar, and hot sesame oil. Serve, topping each bowl of soup with minced scallions.

Calories 85	Total Fat 3 g	Cholesterol 0 mg	Total Carbohydrate 12 g	Protein 3 g
Calories from Fat 25	Saturated Fat 0.5 g	Sodium 270 mg	Dietary Fiber 2 g	Phosphorus 100 mg
	Trans Fat 0 g	Potassium 480 mg	Sugars 3 g	

CHICKEN TORTELLINI SOUP

2 tablespoons olive oil

1 tablespoon minced garlic

10 ounces whole plum tomatoes, peeled and crushed

1 quart low-fat, low-sodium chicken stock

1 cup tortellini pasta

2 tablespoons fresh parsley

1 tablespoon freshly grated Parmesan cheese

1 Heat a medium stockpot over medium heat. Add olive oil and garlic; sweat slightly. Add crushed tomatoes, and bring to a simmer. Continue cooking until liquid is almost completely reduced.

2 Add chicken stock, and bring to a simmer. Add tortellini; cook until tortellini is done.

3 Remove from heat. Add parsley, and serve garnished with Parmesan cheese.

Calories 80	Total Fat 2.5 g	Cholesterol 5 mg	Total Carbohydrate 12 g	Protein 3 g
Calories from Fat 20	Saturated Fat 0.6 g	Sodium 35 mg	Dietary Fiber 1 g	Phosphorus 55 mg
	Trans Fat 0 g	Potassium 255 mg	Sugars 1 g	

ROASTED RED PEPPER AND TOMATO SOUP WITH PESTO

3 medium red bell peppers

1 teaspoon olive oil

1 large onion, diced

3 garlic cloves, minced

Pinch crushed dried red pepper flakes

Salt and pepper to taste

1 (14.5-ounce) can diced tomatoes (fire roasted, if available), drained

1/2 teaspoon dried thyme

1/2 teaspoon sugar

1 cup low-fat, reduced-sodium chicken broth

1/2 cup 1% milk

3 teaspoons commercially prepared pesto

3 tablespoons fat-free sour cream

1 To prepare the peppers, place them whole directly on gas burners set to high. Using tongs, blacken the peppers on all sides. Remove the peppers from the flame, and place in a bowl or Ziploc plastic bag. Cover the bowl with plastic wrap or zip up the bag. Set aside to cool. (For electric stoves and ovens, cut the peppers in half, and discard the seeds and membranes. Place the peppers on a foil-lined broiler pan, skin side up. Broil the peppers in the oven about 4 to 5 inches from the heat source, or until completely blackened. With tongs, remove the peppers and place in a bowl or Ziploc bag. Set aside.)

2 Meanwhile, heat the oil over medium heat. Sauté the onion and garlic for 5 to 6 minutes. Add the crushed red pepper, and season with a little salt and pepper. Add the onion and garlic to a blender or food processor.

3 Once peppers are cooled, peel them by removing the charred skin with your fingers. Cut open each pepper, and discard the seeds and membrane (if you have broiled the peppers as noted above, you will skip this). Tear the peppers into four pieces, and add to the onion and garlic. Process the mixture until smooth. Add in the canned tomatoes, but only pulse with the food processor or blender once or twice, just enough to puree the tomatoes a bit while leaving visible pieces of tomato.

4 Add the pepper-tomato puree to a saucepot. Add in the thyme and sugar and stir. Add in the chicken broth and bring to a slow boil. Lower the heat to medium low and simmer for 15 minutes.

5 Add in the milk, and continue to simmer for 5 to 6 minutes. Season with salt and pepper.

6 To serve, ladle the soup into individual bowls. Top with 1 teaspoon of pesto per serving, and decorate with fat-free sour cream.

Calories 145 Calories from Fat 35	**Total Fat 4 g** Saturated Fat 0.8 g Trans Fat 0 g	**Cholesterol 0 mg** **Sodium 450 mg*** **Potassium 625 mg**	**Total Carbohydrate 24 g** Dietary Fiber 4 g Sugars 14 g	**Protein 5 g** **Phosphorus 115 mg**

*without added salt

SHRIMP AND SHERRY BISQUE

2 pounds shell-on shrimp

1 tablespoon butter

2 medium onions, diced

2 medium carrots, peeled and diced

2 medium celery stalks, diced

2 tablespoons tomato paste

2 medium bay leaves

1/2 teaspoon crushed red pepper flakes

1/2 teaspoon minced fresh tarragon

5 cups water

4 tablespoons flour

1/4 cup dry sherry plus 2 tablespoons

2/3 cup 1% milk

1/2 cup half-and-half

Kosher salt and fresh-ground black pepper to taste

1 Peel the shrimp, and reserve the shells. Devein the shrimp, and then coarsely chop the shrimp into bite-sized pieces, about 1 inch long. Place in the refrigerator until ready to use.

2 Melt the butter in a 5-quart pot over medium heat. Add the onions, carrots, celery, and reserved shrimp shells. Season with salt and pepper, if desired. Cook until shells are tender, about 5 minutes.

3 Add the tomato paste, bay leaves, crushed red pepper flakes, and tarragon, and cook for 1 minute. Add the water, and bring to a boil. Reduce the heat to low, and simmer uncovered for about 45 minutes or until the broth has acquired the flavor of the shrimp and aromatics. Strain through a fine sieve, set aside liquid, and discard solids.

4 Mix together the flour and sherry, and whisk until smooth. Return the shrimp stock to the pot, and slowly add the sherry-flour mixture, whisking constantly. Bring to a boil. Lower the heat and add in the milk, half-and-half, and reserved chopped shrimp. Cook for about 7 to 8 minutes on low heat. Season with salt and pepper. Remove the pot from the heat.

5 Add about 3/4 cup of shrimp and 1 cup of liquid to a food processor or blender, and process until the mixture is smooth. Add pureed mixture back to the pot. Stir in, then serve.

77

Calories 125	Total Fat 3.5 g	Cholesterol 140 mg	Total Carbohydrate 7 g	Protein 16 g
Calories from Fat 30	Saturated Fat 1.8 g	Sodium 680 mg*	Dietary Fiber 1 g	Phosphorus 245 mg
	Trans Fat 0 g	Potassium 250 mg	Sugars 2 g	

*without added salt

CUBAN BLACK BEAN SOUP

2 cups dried black beans, rinsed and picked over

2 slices lean, center-cut bacon, chopped

3 garlic cloves, minced

1 large onion, minced

1 large red bell pepper, cored and diced

1/2 teaspoon ground cumin

1/2 teaspoon dried oregano

1/4 teaspoon dried thyme leaves

6 cups low-fat, reduced-sodium chicken broth

1 (14.5-ounce) can diced tomatoes, undrained

1 tablespoon fresh lime juice

Hot pepper sauce to taste*

Kosher salt and fresh-ground black pepper to taste

1/2 cup nonfat sour cream or nonfat plain Greek-style yogurt for garnish

Not included in nutritional analysis.

1 Place the black beans in a large saucepan, and cover completely with water. Bring to a boil and boil for 2 minutes. Cover and set aside off heat to soak for at least 1 hour or overnight.

2 Drain and rinse the beans under cold water, and set aside.

3 Add the chopped bacon to a 5-quart pot, and cook over medium heat until crisp. Remove the bacon pieces with a slotted spoon and set aside.

4 Add the garlic, onions, and red peppers to the pot. Sauté over medium heat for about 7 to 8 minutes until the vegetables are lightly browned. Add in the cumin, oregano, and thyme. Sauté for 1 minute.

5 Add in the broth, tomatoes, and reserved black beans. Bring to a boil. Lower the heat, and simmer, partially covered, for 1 hour or until the beans are tender.

6 Remove the pot from the heat. Add about 2 cups of the bean soup to a food processor or blender, and process until the mixture is smooth. Add pureed mixture back in the pot. Add in the lime juice and hot sauce. Season with salt and pepper.

7 To serve: Top each bowl with some reserved bacon pieces and a dollop of sour cream or yogurt.

79

Calories 245	Total Fat 4.5 g	Cholesterol 5 mg	Total Carbohydrate 39 g	Protein 15 g
Calories from Fat 40	Saturated Fat 1.5 g	Sodium 520 mg*	Dietary Fiber 12 g	Phosphorus 240 mg
	Trans Fat 0 g	Potassium 775 mg	Sugars 7 g	

*without added salt

MEXICAN-STYLE MEAT CHILI

2 teaspoons cumin seeds

2 teaspoons coriander seeds

1 tablespoon canola oil

2 pounds lean boneless chuck roast, cubed, or lean ground beef (95–96% lean)

1 large onion, chopped

6 garlic cloves, minced

3 jalapeño peppers, seeded and minced (leave the seeds if you prefer more heat)

1 tablespoon dried oregano

1 (28-ounce) can whole tomatoes with liquid, coarsely chopped

1 (12-ounce) bottle dark beer

1 ounce unsweetened chocolate, grated

3 cups low-fat, reduced-sodium chicken broth

Sea salt and fresh-ground black pepper to taste

1 In a small skillet, toast the cumin and coriander seeds over medium heat for 3 to 4 minutes until fragrant. Using a coffee or spice grinder, grind the seeds into a powder. Set aside.

2 Heat the canola oil in a large Dutch oven or other heavy lidded pot over medium-high heat. Add the beef and brown, about 5 to 6 minutes. Remove the beef with a slotted spoon to a bowl and set aside.

3 Add the onions, garlic, and jalapeño peppers to the skillet, and sauté for 4 to 5 minutes. Add in the ground cumin and coriander and the dried oregano. Cook for 2 minutes. Add the beef back in, and add the tomatoes, beer, chocolate, and broth. Bring to a boil. Lower the heat and simmer for 20 to 25 minutes. Season with salt and pepper, and serve.

Calories 210	**Total Fat 8 g**	**Cholesterol 55 mg**	**Total Carbohydrate 10 g**	**Protein 21 g**
Calories from Fat 70	Saturated Fat 2.9 g	**Sodium 340 mg***	Dietary Fiber 2 g	**Phosphorus 215 mg**
	Trans Fat 0 g	**Potassium 500 mg**	Sugars 4 g	

*without added salt

WHITE BEAN CHICKEN CHILI

POACHED CHICKEN

- 1/2 pound boneless skinless chicken breast
- Water to cover
- 4 whole black peppercorns

CHILI

- 1 tablespoon olive oil
- 1 large onion, chopped
- 2 garlic cloves, minced
- 1 jalapeño pepper, seeded and minced
- 2 teaspoons ground cumin
- 1 1/2 teaspoons dried oregano
- 1 teaspoon mild chili powder
- 1 teaspoon ground coriander
- 1/8 teaspoon ground cloves
- 1/4 teaspoon cayenne
- 2 (15-ounce) cans no-salt-added navy beans, drained and rinsed
- 3 cups low-fat, reduced-sodium chicken broth
- 1/2 cup reduced-fat Monterey Jack cheese
- Sea salt and fresh-ground pepper to taste
- 2 teaspoons fresh lime juice

1 To poach the chicken: Place the chicken breasts in a skillet with a tight-fitting lid. Add water to cover the top of the chicken, and add the peppercorns. Bring the water to a boil. Lower the heat to simmer, cover, and let the chicken poach for about 8 to 10 minutes until it is completely cooked through and no traces of pink remain. With a slotted spoon, remove the chicken from the skillet and place on a plate to cool. Set aside.

2 Heat the oil in a saucepan over medium-high heat. Add the onions and garlic, and sauté for about 6 minutes, or until onions are translucent. Add the jalapeño pepper, and sauté for 3 minutes. Add the cumin, oregano, chili powder, coriander, cloves, and cayenne; sauté for 2 minutes. Add the beans and broth, and bring to a boil. Lower the heat and simmer for 20 minutes.

3 Dice the chicken breast and add to the chili. Heat for 5 minutes. Remove the pan from the heat and add the cheese. Adjust the seasoning with salt and pepper. Add the lime juice and serve.

Calories 370	**Total Fat 9 g**	**Cholesterol 40 mg**	**Total Carbohydrate 44 g**	**Protein 31 g**
Calories from Fat 80	Saturated Fat 2.8 g	**Sodium 555 mg***	Dietary Fiber 14 g	**Phosphorus 380 mg**
	Trans Fat 0 g	**Potassium 695 mg**	Sugars 4 g	

*without added salt

SOUPS

CHICKPEA SOUP WITH MINI MEATBALLS

2 teaspoons olive oil

1 large carrot, diced

1 large onion, diced

2 celery stalks, diced

2 garlic cloves, minced

2 teaspoons dried rosemary

2 (15-ounce) cans chickpeas, drained and rinsed

3 1/2 cups low-fat, reduced-sodium chicken broth

1 (14.5-ounce) can diced tomatoes

Salt and pepper to taste

MINI MEATBALLS

1/2 pound lean (93%) ground beef

2 1/2 tablespoons plain dry bread crumbs

2 tablespoons cold water

1 garlic clove, minced

1 scallion, minced

Salt and pepper to taste

1 Heat the oil in a large pot over medium heat. Reduce the heat to medium low. Add the carrot, onion, and celery, and sauté for 7 to 8 minutes. Add the garlic and rosemary, and sauté for 2 minutes.

2 Add in the chickpeas, broth, and tomatoes, and bring to a boil. Lower the heat, and simmer for 25 minutes.

3 Meanwhile, make the meatballs. Combine all the meatball ingredients in a medium bowl, and form into small meatballs, about 1 tablespoon each. Coat a large nonstick skillet with cooking spray over medium-high heat. Add the meatballs and sauté on all sides for 4 to 5 minutes, or until cooked through.

4 Add the meatballs to the soup, and season well with salt and pepper.

Calories 260	Total Fat 7 g	Cholesterol 25 mg	Total Carbohydrate 34 g	Protein 18 g
Calories from Fat 65	Saturated Fat 1.6 g	**Sodium 605 mg***	Dietary Fiber 9 g	**Phosphorus 260 mg**
	Trans Fat 0.1 g	**Potassium 740 mg**	Sugars 9 g	

*without added salt

SOUPS

FRESH GREENS SOUP WITH WHITE BEANS, BASIL, AND TOMATOES

1 1/2 tablespoons olive oil

1 large leek (about 6 ounces), cleaned, white part only, chopped (1/2 cup)

1 medium (6-ounce) onion, chopped (about 1 cup)

4 garlic cloves, minced

2 small carrots, peeled and diced

3 tablespoons minced fresh parsley

1/4 pound green Swiss chard, finely sliced (about 2 1/2 cups)

3 small tomatoes, seeded and diced (about 1 3/4 cups)

6 cups low-sodium vegetable broth

Pinch crushed red pepper flakes

Kosher salt and freshly ground black pepper to taste

1 (15.5-ounce) can white beans, drained

1/4 cup sliced fresh basil

GARNISH

1/4 cup freshly grated Parmesan cheese

1 Heat the oil in a large saucepan over medium heat. Add the leeks, onions, garlic, and carrots, and sauté for about 6 to 7 minutes, or until the onions are soft, stirring occasionally. Add in the parsley, and sauté for 2 minutes.

2 Add in the Swiss chard, and sauté for 2 minutes. Add in the tomatoes, and sauté for 2 minutes. Pour in the broth and the crushed red pepper flakes. Season with salt and pepper. Bring to a boil, lower the heat, and simmer for 10 minutes.

3 Add in the beans and basil, and simmer for 5 minutes. Garnish each bowl with Parmesan cheese.

COOK'S TIP | Can be made a day or two in advance. Garnish just before serving.

Calories 115	Total Fat 4 g	Cholesterol 5 mg	Total Carbohydrate 16 g	Protein 5 g
Calories from Fat 35	Saturated Fat 0.9 g	Sodium 195 mg*	Dietary Fiber 4 g	Phosphorus 120 mg
	Trans Fat 0 g	Potassium 435 mg	Sugars 4 g	

*without added salt

OLD-FASHIONED CHICKEN NOODLE SOUP

STOCK

- 1 rinsed whole chicken (4 pounds), skinned (except for the wings) and cut into parts
- 2 large unpeeled onions, quartered
- 4 medium unpeeled carrots, cut into chunks
- 4 large celery stalks, coarsely chopped
- 6 sprigs fresh parsley
- 6 black peppercorns
- 3 bay leaves
- Salt to taste

SOUP

- 2 teaspoons olive oil
- 1 large onion (10 ounces), chopped
- 2 large carrots, peeled and sliced diagonally into 1/2-inch pieces
- 1 large celery stalk, sliced diagonally into 1/2-inch pieces
- 8 ounces wide egg noodles or linguine (whole wheat if desired)
- Kosher salt and freshly ground black pepper to taste
- 2 tablespoons minced fresh parsley
- 2 teaspoons minced fresh thyme

1 To prepare the stock, place the chicken parts in a heavy stockpot. Add the onions, carrots, and celery. Add in 3 quarts of water, and bring to a boil. Skim the surface to remove any gray residue.

2 Add the parsley, peppercorns, bay leaves, and salt. Partially cover the pan, and simmer on low heat for 1 hour, 20 minutes. Remove the chicken parts, and set aside to cool.

3 Line a large colander with cheesecloth, and strain the broth, pressing on the solids to extract all the juices. Discard the vegetables, and reserve the stock, about 10 cups. Add the stock to a large container, and refrigerate for several hours. When it has cooled, spoon off and discard any solidified fat. The stock should be clear.

4 To prepare the soup, remove and discard all the bones from the chicken parts. Cut about 1 pound of the chicken meat into small pieces for the soup. Save any remaining chicken for another use. Wrap the leftover chicken in an airtight container, and keep in the refrigerator for up to 2 to 3 days.

5 In a large saucepan, heat the olive oil. Add the onion, and sauté for 5 minutes. Add the carrots and celery, and sauté for 5 minutes. Add in the reserved stock, and bring to a boil. Add the egg noodles or linguine, reduce the heat to medium, and simmer for 6 to 7 minutes. Stir in the cooked chicken. Season the soup lightly with salt and black pepper. Sprinkle in fresh minced parsley and thyme.

Calories 150	Total Fat 4 g	Cholesterol 45 mg	Total Carbohydrate 15 g	Protein 13 g
Calories from Fat 35	Saturated Fat 1.1 g	Sodium 55 mg*	Dietary Fiber 1 g	Phosphorus 115 mg
	Trans Fat 0 g	Potassium 205 mg	Sugars 2 g	

*without added salt

BUTTERNUT SQUASH AND LEEK SOUP

1 large (about 3 pounds) butternut squash

2 cups chopped, well-washed leeks, white part only (about 2 medium)

1/4 cup dry white wine

4 1/2 cups low-fat, reduced-sodium chicken broth

1 teaspoon ground white pepper

1/2 teaspoon kosher salt

1 tablespoon butter

TOPPING

3 tablespoons chopped pistachios

1/2 cup plain nonfat yogurt

1/4 cup crème fraîche (a heavy cream thickened with buttermilk)

1 tablespoon minced fresh chive

1 Place the butternut squash in a microwave oven (on the glass turntable or the rack). Microwave the squash on high for 5 to 6 minutes. Remove the squash carefully with pot holders, and set aside until it is cool enough to handle. Microwaving makes it easier to cut the squash. If you don't have a microwave oven or want to skip this step, proceed with step 2.

2 Cut the squash in half crosswise. Standing each piece upright, carefully peel the skin off with a sharp knife or vegetable peeler. Discard the skin. Set each piece of squash lengthwise on a cutting board. Cut each piece in half lengthwise. Remove and discard the seeds from the squash. Using a serrated spoon, remove any excess stringy fibers from the squash. Cut all the squash into 1-inch cubes. You should have about 10 cups of cubes.

3 Add the squash and leeks to a large, heavy saucepot. Add in the wine and broth. Cover and bring to a boil over medium-high heat. Reduce to a simmer and cook until the squash is tender, about 25 minutes. Let cool for 15 minutes. Add in the white pepper and salt.

4 Puree the soup, in batches if necessary, in a food processor or blender (use an immersion blender if you have one). Add the soup back to the saucepot, and add the butter. Set over low heat for a few minutes, just until the butter melts.

5 For the topping, toast the pistachios in a small, dry skillet for 2 to 3 minutes, shaking the pan frequently, until they are lightly browned. Set aside. In a small bowl, combine the yogurt, crème fraîche, and chives. For each bowl of soup, swirl the yogurt mixture on top. Top with the chopped pistachios.

Calories 115	**Total Fat 5 g**	**Cholesterol 10 mg**	**Total Carbohydrate 15 g**	**Protein 4 g**
Calories from Fat 45	Saturated Fat 2.4 g	**Sodium 395 mg**	Dietary Fiber 4 g	**Phosphorus 85 mg**
	Trans Fat 0.1 g	**Potassium 435 mg**	Sugars 4 g	

SOUPS

SPICED PORK STEW

1 dried ancho pepper, seeded

2 tablespoons all-purpose flour

2 pounds boneless pork loin shoulder, trimmed of excess fat, cut into 1/2-inch cubes

2 tablespoons olive oil, divided

1 large onion, chopped

3 garlic cloves, minced

1 small red bell pepper, cored, seeded, and diced

1 teaspoon ground cumin

1/2 teaspoon dried oregano leaves

1 (28-ounce) can whole tomatoes

2 cups low-fat, reduced-sodium chicken broth

1 tablespoon unsweetened cocoa

1 (15-ounce) can kidney beans, drained and rinsed

Kosher salt and freshly ground black pepper to taste

GARNISH

1/4 cup chopped fresh cilantro

1 Place the ancho chili pepper in a small bowl with boiling water to cover. Set aside for 20 minutes.

2 Add the flour to a large bowl. Dry the pork cubes well with paper towels. Toss the pork cubes with the flour until lightly coated, shaking off any excess flour.

3 Heat a large Dutch oven over medium-high heat. Add 1 tablespoon of the olive oil to the pan. Add the pork, in batches if needed, and sauté for about 5 to 7 minutes until well browned. Remove the pork from the skillet with a slotted spoon.

4 Add the remaining oil to the pan, and reduce the heat to medium low. Add in the onions, and sauté for about 10 minutes. Raise the heat to medium, and add the garlic, red peppers, cumin, and oregano. Sauté for about 4 minutes, or until the vegetables are soft. Add the pork back to the pot.

5 Add the whole tomatoes to a large bowl. Crush the tomatoes coarsely with your hands. Remove the ancho chili from the water and chop finely. Add the chili, tomatoes, and broth to the pot, and bring to a boil. Cover and simmer on low for about 2 hours, or until the pork is tender.

6 Remove about 1/2 cup of the cooking liquid from the pot, and add to a small bowl. Add in the cocoa and whisk well. Add the cocoa mixture to the pot. Add in the beans, and simmer uncovered for 5 to 7 minutes. Some of the liquid will evaporate, thickening the stew. Season with salt and pepper. Garnish with cilantro.

COOK'S TIP | This stew's flavor is really complex but mild. For a spicier stew, add 1/4 teaspoon or more of cayenne pepper along with the cumin and oregano.

Calories 275	Total Fat 11 g	Cholesterol 50 mg	Total Carbohydrate 19 g	Protein 26 g
Calories from Fat 100	Saturated Fat 3.5 g	Sodium 360 mg*	Dietary Fiber 5 g	Phosphorus 225 mg
	Trans Fat 0 g	Potassium 765 mg	Sugars 5 g	
			*without added salt	

OLD-FASHIONED BEEF STEW

2 tablespoons all-purpose flour

2 pounds boneless lean beef chuck steak

3 tablespoons olive oil, divided

2 large portobello mushrooms, cleaned, stemmed, and cut into 1/2-inch pieces

4 large carrots, peeled and thickly sliced on the diagonal

2 cups frozen pearl onions, thawed and patted dry

2 small red potatoes, unpeeled, washed, and cut into 1-inch cubes

2 garlic cloves, minced

1 1/2 cups dark beer

2 cups reduced-sodium, low-fat beef broth

4 sprigs fresh thyme, chopped

1 sprig fresh rosemary, chopped

Kosher salt and freshly ground black pepper to taste

GARNISH

1/4 cup minced fresh parsley

1 Add the flour to a large bowl. Pat the beef very well with paper towels. Add in the beef and toss gently. Shake off any excess flour.

2 Heat 2 tablespoons of the oil in a large Dutch oven. Add the beef, in batches, and cook until browned on all sides, about 5 to 7 minutes. Remove the beef with a slotted spoon and set aside.

3 Add the remaining 1 tablespoon of oil to the pot, and add in the portobello mushrooms. Sauté the mushrooms for about 5 to 6 minutes until browned. Remove the mushrooms with a slotted spoon, and set aside on a plate. Add in the carrots, pearl onions, and red potatoes, and sauté for 5 to 6 minutes. Add in the garlic, and sauté for 3 minutes. Remove the vegetables with a slotted spoon to a bowl and set aside.

4 Add the beef back to the pot. Add in the beer, and simmer over medium heat for about 8 minutes. Add in the beef broth, and bring to a boil. Reduce the heat to low, cover, and simmer for about 1 hour, or until the beef is very tender. Add in the carrots, onions, and potatoes, cover, and simmer for another 45 minutes to 1 hour, until the vegetables are soft.

5 Add in the mushrooms, thyme, and rosemary, and simmer uncovered for 5 to 7 minutes. Some of the liquid will evaporate, thickening the stew. Season with salt and pepper. Garnish with parsley.

95

Calories 170	Total Fat 7 g	Cholesterol 40 mg	Total Carbohydrate 11 g	Protein 16 g
Calories from Fat 65	Saturated Fat 1.8 g	Sodium 145 mg*	Dietary Fiber 2 g	Phosphorus 170 mg
	Trans Fat 0.2 g	Potassium 465 mg	Sugars 3 g	

*without added salt

LENTIL CHILI

4 dried guajillo chilies, stemmed and seeded

4 dried pasilla chilies, stemmed and seeded

1/2 teaspoon cumin seeds

1/2 teaspoon coriander seeds

1 tablespoon coarsely chopped fresh oregano

2 small onions, chopped

3 garlic cloves, minced

1 (28-ounce) can whole tomatoes with liquid

1 tablespoon olive oil

1 1/2 cups bulgur wheat

1 cup dried brown lentils

2 1/2 cups water

1 (15-ounce) can red kidney beans, drained and rinsed

1 In a large skillet, toast the guajillo and pasilla chilies on each side until browned, about 2 minutes. Be careful not to burn the peppers. Transfer the chilies to a bowl. Pour boiling water over them, and let stand for 30 minutes.

2 Meanwhile, heat a skillet over medium-high heat. Add the cumin and coriander seeds and toast for 5 minutes, until fragrant. Using a coffee or spice grinder, grind the seeds into a powder. Add the oregano to the skillet and toast for 3 minutes. Set aside.

3 Reserve 1 cup of liquid from the soaked chilies and discard the rest. Place the rehydrated chilies and the reserved 1 cup of water into a blender or food processor. Add the ground cumin and coriander seeds, toasted oregano, onions, garlic, and tomatoes with their liquid. Puree until smooth.

4 Heat the olive oil in a saucepan over medium heat. Add the bulgur wheat and lentils, and cook for about 5 minutes. Add the chili mixture and the 2 1/2 cups of water. Bring to a boil, lower the heat, and simmer for 30 minutes or until lentils are tender. Add in the kidney beans. Simmer 5 minutes more before serving.

Calories 255	Total Fat 3.5 g	Cholesterol 0 mg	Total Carbohydrate 46 g	Protein 14 g
Calories from Fat 30	Saturated Fat 0.4 g	Sodium 215 mg	Dietary Fiber 14 g	Phosphorus 250 mg
	Trans Fat 0 g	Potassium 836 mg	Sugars 5 g	

VEGETABLES

ROASTED WINTER ROOT VEGETABLES

2 tablespoons olive oil

1 cup peeled carrots, cut into 1 1/2-inch chunks

1 cup sweet potatoes, peeled, cut into 1 1/2-inch chunks

1 cup peeled parsnips, cut into 1 1/2-inch chunks

1 cup peeled turnips, cut into 1 1/2-inch chunks

3 shallots, peeled, left whole

6 whole garlic cloves, unpeeled

Salt and pepper to taste

1 Preheat the oven to 425°F.

2 In a large bowl, combine all the ingredients and toss well. Spread the vegetables in one layer onto a large baking sheet.

3 Roast for about 30 minutes, shaking the pan and tossing the vegetables every 10 minutes. Continue to roast longer if necessary so that the vegetables are soft and brown. If the vegetables become soft before they brown, increase the heat to 450°F. If they brown before they become soft, add a few tablespoons of water and lower the temperature to 375°F.

99

Calories 85	Total Fat 3.5 g	Cholesterol 0 mg	Total Carbohydrate 13 g	Protein 1 g
Calories from Fat 30	Saturated Fat 0.5 g	**Sodium 20 mg***	Dietary Fiber 2 g	**Phosphorus 40 mg**
	Trans Fat 0 g	**Potassium 255 mg**	Sugars 3 g	

without added salt

VEGETABLES

RUTABAGA AND CARROT HASH

1 pound peeled rutabaga, quartered and thinly sliced

1/2 pound baking potatoes, peeled and thinly sliced

1 1/2 pounds carrots, peeled and thinly sliced

5 garlic cloves, peeled

1 bay leaf

Salt and pepper to taste

2 cups reduced-sodium, low-fat chicken broth

2 cups water

1 tablespoon olive oil

1 In a large saucepan combine the rutabaga, potatoes, carrots, garlic, bay leaf, salt and pepper to taste, broth, and water. Bring to a boil over medium heat, reduce to a simmer, cover, and cook for 30 minutes until tender. Drain the vegetables, reserving 1/2 cup liquid. Remove and discard the bay leaf.

2 With a potato masher, mash the vegetables with the reserved cooking liquid and the olive oil. Readjust seasonings if necessary and serve.

101

Calories 65	Total Fat 1.5 g	Cholesterol 0 mg	Total Carbohydrate 12 g	Protein 2 g
Calories from Fat 15	Saturated Fat 0.2 g	Sodium 90 mg*	Dietary Fiber 3 g	Phosphorus 50 mg
	Trans Fat 0 g	Potassium 360 mg	Sugars 5 g	

*without added salt

SESAME KALE WITH GARLIC AND GINGER

2 teaspoons sesame oil, divided

3 garlic cloves, thinly sliced

1 tablespoon finely grated ginger

2 large bunches kale, washed, ribs removed, coarsely chopped

2 tablespoons water

1 tablespoon toasted sesame seeds

2 teaspoons light soy sauce

Dash crushed red pepper flakes

1 In a wok or skillet, heat 1 teaspoon of the sesame oil over medium heat. Add the garlic and ginger and sauté for 1 minute. Add the kale, in batches, and sauté for 2 minutes. Add the water, cover, and steam until the kale wilts but is still slightly crunchy.

2 Top the kale with sesame seeds, soy sauce, and remaining sesame oil, and mix to combine. Add a dash of crushed red pepper flakes if desired.

103

Calories 50	Total Fat 2.5 g	Cholesterol 0 mg	Total Carbohydrate 6 g	Protein 2 g
Calories from Fat 20	Saturated Fat 0.4 g	Sodium 85 mg	Dietary Fiber 2 g	Phosphorus 40 mg
	Trans Fat 0 g	Potassium 230 mg	Sugars 1 g	

VEGETABLES

ROASTED KOHLRABI

2 pounds kohlrabi, peeled and cut into large chunks

1 tablespoon olive oil

1 tablespoon minced garlic

Salt and pepper to taste

Balsamic vinegar (optional, for drizzling over dish; not included in nutritional analysis)

1 Preheat the oven to 450°F. In a bowl, combine all the ingredients other than balsamic vinegar, and toss well.

2 Arrange the kohlrabi in a single layer on a baking sheet. Roast the kohlrabi for about 30 to 35 minutes, stirring every 10 minutes or so to prevent burning.

3 Drizzle with balsamic vinegar if desired.

Calories 50	Total Fat 2.5 g	Cholesterol 0 mg	Total Carbohydrate 7 g	Protein 2 g
Calories from Fat 20	Saturated Fat 0.3 g	Sodium 20 mg*	Dietary Fiber 1 g	Phosphorus 45 mg
	Trans Fat 0 g	Potassium 330 mg	Sugars 3 g	

*without added salt

VEGETABLES

STEWED CHAYOTE SQUASH

1 pound chayote squash
1 tablespoon olive oil
1 medium onion, chopped
2 cloves garlic, thinly sliced
1 large tomato, chopped
1/2 to 1 canned chipotle chili in adobo sauce, minced
1/2 cup fat-free sour cream
1/2 ounce freshly grated parmesan cheese

1 Peel and pit the chayote squash; cut into small chunks. Heat the oil over medium heat. Add the onion and garlic; cook for 5 minutes, stirring often.

2 Add the squash, tomato, and chili. Reduce the heat, cover, and simmer for about 30 minutes. Remove from the heat, and stir in the sour cream. Sprinkle with Parmesan cheese.

Calories 105	**Total Fat 5 g**	**Cholesterol 5 mg**	**Total Carbohydrate 13 g**	**Protein 4 g**
Calories from Fat 45	Saturated Fat 1.2 g	**Sodium 90 mg**	Dietary Fiber 3 g	**Phosphorus 90 mg**
	Trans Fat 0 g	**Potassium 335 mg**	Sugars 5 g	

ROASTED CELERY ROOT AND BABY CARROTS

1 whole (1 pound) celery root, peeled and diced into 1-inch cubes

2 tablespoons olive oil, divided

1 teaspoon salt, divided

Pinch of black pepper, divided

2 sprigs fresh rosemary, about 1 inch long

1/2 pound baby carrots

1 Place diced celery root in a medium bowl. Add 1 tablespoon olive oil, 1/2 teaspoon salt, black pepper, and fresh rosemary; toss until fully coated. Place in a baking dish, and bake at 375°F for about 45 minutes or until golden brown.

2 Place the carrots in a medium bowl. Add 1 tablespoon olive oil, 1/2 teaspoon salt, and black pepper; toss until fully coated. Place in a baking dish, and bake at 375°F for about 30 minutes, or until fully cooked. Begin baking carrots 15 minutes after putting celery in the oven to ensure equal cooking times.

3 When both dishes are done, combine in a serving bowl, and serve hot.

109

Calories 65	**Total Fat 3.5 g**	**Cholesterol 0 mg**	**Total Carbohydrate 8 g**	**Protein 1 g**
Calories from Fat 30	Saturated Fat 0.5 g	**Sodium 365 mg**	Dietary Fiber 2 g	**Phosphorus 75 mg**
	Trans Fat 0 g	**Potassium 265 mg**	Sugars 2 g	

VEGETABLES

GARDEN-FRESH GREEN BEANS WITH BALSAMIC RED ONION

BALSAMIC RED ONION

- 1 large red onion, halved, peeled, and sliced into 1/4-inch-thick pieces
- 2 teaspoons olive oil
- 2 teaspoons balsamic vinegar

  Kosher salt and fresh-ground black pepper to taste

GREEN BEANS

- 1 pound fresh green beans, trimmed
- 1 1/2 teaspoons olive oil

1 Prepare the red onion: Preheat the oven to 400°F. Toss the red onion pieces with the 2 teaspoons olive oil, balsamic vinegar, salt, and pepper. Place the onions in a single layer on a baking sheet lined with parchment paper. Roast for about 25 to 30 minutes, shaking the pan occasionally until the onions are very tender and deep in color.

2 Meanwhile, bring a pot of lightly salted water to a boil. Add the green beans, turn off the heat, and let them stand in the water for about 2 minutes. Drain and run under cold water; drain again.

3 Heat the olive oil in a large skillet. Add the green beans, and sauté for 3 to 5 minutes. Add the roasted red onions, and cook for 2 to 3 minutes. Taste and correct the seasonings, if needed.

Calories 45	Total Fat 2.0 g	Cholesterol 0 mg	Total Carbohydrate 7 g	Protein 1 g
Calories from Fat 20	Saturated Fat 0.3 g	**Sodium 0 mg***	Dietary Fiber 2 g	**Phosphorus 20 mg**
	Trans Fat 0 g	**Potassium 115 mg**	Sugars 2 g	

*without added salt

FOUR-MUSHROOM SALAD

2 tablespoons olive oil

1 1/2 pounds mixed fresh mushrooms (at least four varieties, such as button, cremini, shiitake, and trumpet), quartered or roughly chopped

1/2 cup dry white wine

2 garlic cloves, minced

1 1/2 tablespoons chopped parsley

1 tablespoon chopped fresh thyme

1 tablespoon lemon juice

1/2 teaspoon salt or to taste

1/4 teaspoon black pepper

2 tablespoons freshly grated Parmesan cheese

1 Heat the olive oil in a saute pan on high heat.

2 Add the mushrooms, and cook for 4 to 5 minutes or until they begin to brown. Stir in the white wine, cover the pan, and cook for 2 minutes.

3 Remove the cover, and cook until the liquid is reduced by half.

4 Transfer the mushrooms and their juices to a bowl, and stir in garlic, parsley, thyme, lemon juice, salt, and pepper.

5 Let the mushrooms cool to room temperature. Divide among 4 salad plates. Sprinkle with cheese.

Calories 130	Total Fat 8 g	Cholesterol 5 mg	Total Carbohydrate 9 g	Protein 6 g
Calories from Fat 70	Saturated Fat 1.5 g	Sodium 330 mg	Dietary Fiber 2 g	Phosphorus 195 mg
	Trans Fat 0 g	Potassium 670 mg	Sugars 3 g	

VEGETABLES

HERBED SNAP PEA TOSS

1 pound baby carrots

1 pound sugar snap peas

1 tablespoon olive oil

2 large shallots, sliced

1 1/2 teaspoons minced fresh thyme

Kosher salt and fresh-ground black pepper to taste

1/2 teaspoon fresh lemon zest (optional, not included in nutritional analysis)

1 In a large skillet over high heat, bring 1 inch of lightly salted water to a boil. Add the carrots, and cook for 5 minutes. Add the snap peas, cover, and cook for 2 minutes. Drain, remove carrots and peas, and set aside. Wipe out the skillet.

2 Add the olive oil to the pan, add the shallots, and sauté for 5 minutes. Add in the fresh thyme, and cook for 2 minutes. Stir in the carrots, snap peas, salt, and pepper. Cook for 1 to 2 minutes, until heated through.

115

Calories 45	Total Fat 1.5 g	Cholesterol 0 mg	Total Carbohydrate 8 g	Protein 1 g
Calories from Fat 15	Saturated Fat 0.2 g	Sodium 45 mg	Dietary Fiber 2 g	Phosphorus 35 mg
	Trans Fat 0 g	Potassium 185 mg	Sugars 3 g	

VEGETABLES

ZESTY BROCCOLINI AND GARLIC

1 tablespoon olive oil

4 garlic cloves, thinly sliced

2 pounds broccolini, stems trimmed

1/4 cup low-sodium vegetable broth

Pinch crushed red pepper

Kosher salt and freshly ground black pepper to taste

1 1/2 tablespoons fresh lemon juice

2 teaspoons fresh lemon zest

1 Heat the oil over medium-low heat. Add the garlic, and sauté for about 5 to 6 minutes, or just until the garlic starts to brown. Add in the broccolini, broth, crushed red pepper, salt, and black pepper. Cover the pan, and let it steam on medium-high heat until the broccolini turns bright green and is tender, about 5 to 6 minutes.

2 Add in the lemon juice and zest, and serve immediately.

Calories 60	Total Fat 2 g	Cholesterol 0 mg	Total Carbohydrate 8 g	Protein 4 g
Calories from Fat 20	Saturated Fat 0.3 g	**Sodium 35 mg***	Dietary Fiber 1 g	**Phosphorus 70 mg**
	Trans Fat 0 g	**Potassium 350 mg**	Sugars 2 g	

*without added salt

VEGETABLES

CRUNCHY SNOW PEA SALAD WITH JICAMA AND CHERRY TOMATOES

1 cup washed, trimmed fresh snow peas

5 large radishes, trimmed (about 1/2 cup)

1/2 medium peeled jicama (about 3/4 cup)

1 cup cherry tomatoes

2 cups washed, chopped romaine lettuce

DRESSING

2 tablespoons fresh lemon juice

1 garlic clove, minced (1 teaspoon)

1/2 teaspoon Dijon mustard

3 tablespoons olive oil

1/4 teaspoon kosher salt

Freshly ground black pepper to taste

1 Slice each snow pea in thirds on the diagonal. Cut each radish in half and then thinly slice. Slice the jicama into 1/2-inch-wide strips, then cut into 1/2-inch cubes. Cut each cherry tomato in half.

2 Place the snow peas, radishes, jicama, and cherry tomatoes in a bowl. Add the romaine lettuce and toss.

3 In a small bowl, whisk together the dressing ingredients and add to the vegetables. Toss again and serve.

119

Calories 125	Total Fat 10 g	Cholesterol 0 mg	Total Carbohydrate 7 g	Protein 2 g
Calories from Fat 90	Saturated Fat 1.4 g	Sodium 150 mg	Dietary Fiber 3 g	Phosphorus 40 mg
	Trans Fat 0 g	Potassium 275 mg	Sugars 3 g	

SIDES

INCA RED QUINOA PILAF

2 teaspoons olive oil

1/2 cup chopped onion

2 teaspoons minced ginger

2 garlic cloves, minced

1 cup Inca Red quinoa

1 1/2 cups low-fat, reduced-sodium chicken broth

1 cup canned chickpeas, rinsed and drained

1/3 cup raisins, plumped in hot water for 10 minutes, then drained

1 tablespoon minced fresh mint

2 tablespoons lime juice

Salt and black pepper to taste

1 Heat the oil in a large skillet over medium heat. Add the onion, ginger, and garlic, and saute for 4 minutes. Add the quinoa, and sauté 1 minute.

2 Add the broth, and bring to a boil. Lower the heat, cover, and cook for 15 minutes. Fluff the quinoa with a fork, and add the chickpeas, raisins, mint, and lime juice. Season with salt and pepper. Cook for 1 minute.

Calories 180	Total Fat 3.5 g	Cholesterol 0 mg	Total Carbohydrate 32 g	Protein 6 g
Calories from Fat 30	Saturated Fat 0.4 g	Sodium 150 mg*	Dietary Fiber 6 g	Phosphorus 180 mg
	Trans Fat 0 g	Potassium 330 mg	Sugars 8 g	

*without added salt

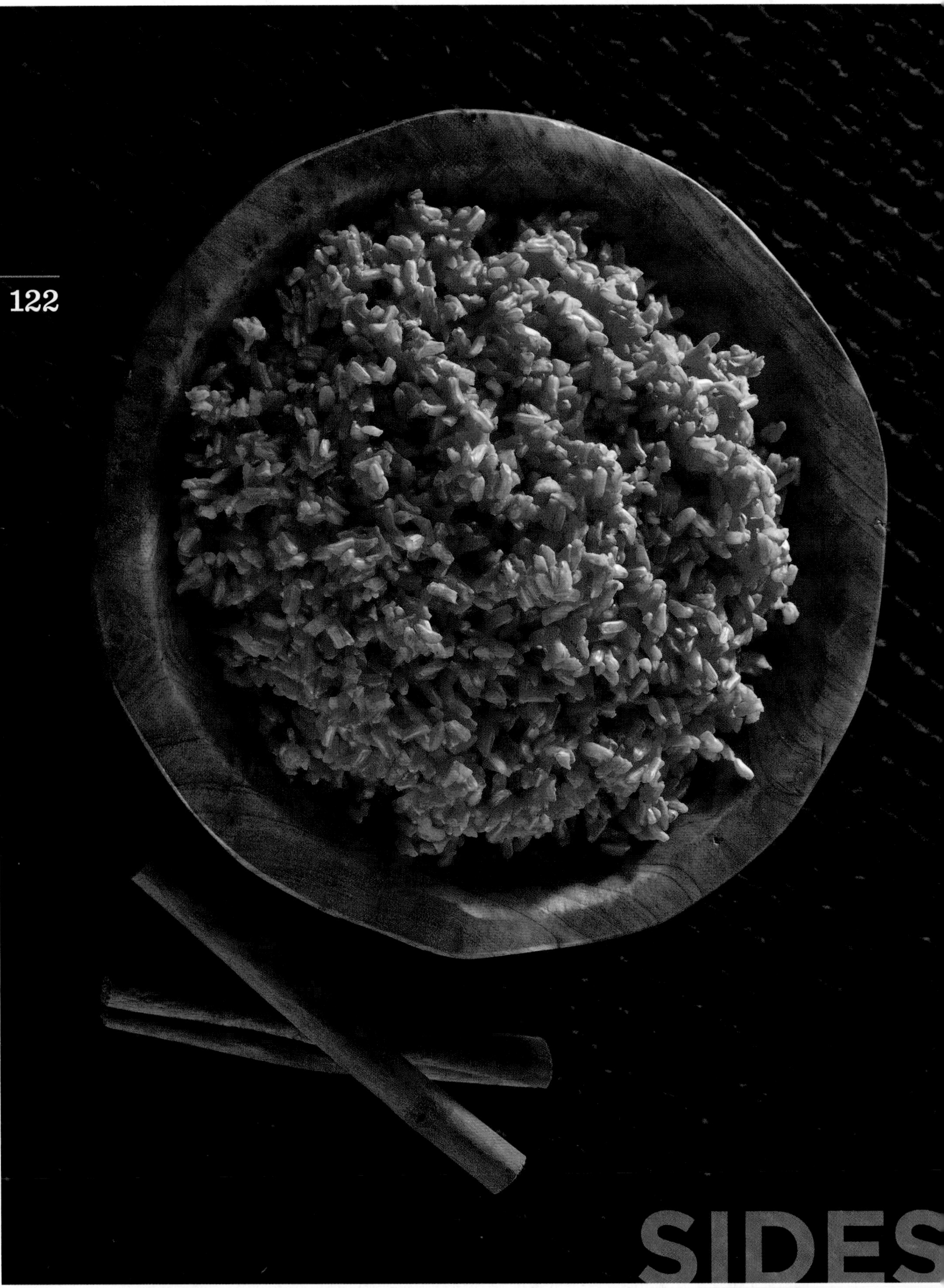
SIDES

CINNAMON AND CARDAMOM BROWN RICE

2 cups water

1 (1-inch) piece cinnamon stick

1 cardamom pod

Pinch salt

1 whole clove

Large pinch saffron threads

1 cup brown basmati rice, rinsed for 1 minute in a fine sieve

1 In medium saucepan, bring water, cinnamon, cardamom, salt, clove, and saffron threads to a boil. Add the rice, lower the heat, cover, and simmer for about 45 minutes until rice is tender.

2 Remove the whole spices before serving.

Calories 160	Total Fat 1.5 g	Cholesterol 0 mg	Total Carbohydrate 34 g	Protein 4 g
Calories from Fat 15	Saturated Fat 0.3 g	Sodium 35 mg	Dietary Fiber 2 g	Phosphorus 120 mg
	Trans Fat 0.3 g	Potassium 65 mg	Sugars 1 g	

SIDES

CREAMY CHEESY CAULIFLOWER ✓

10 cups coarsely chopped cauliflower, about 2 heads

2 teaspoons butter

2 large onions, chopped

3 garlic cloves, minced

1/2 cup all-purpose flour

3 1/2 cups 1% milk

Salt and pepper to taste

3/4 cup freshly grated Parmesan cheese

3 tablespoons finely minced parsley

1 Add 4 quarts of water to a 6-quart saucepan. Bring the water to a boil. Add the cauliflower, and cook for about 10 to 12 minutes or until tender. Drain. Set aside.

2 In a large skillet, melt the butter over medium-high heat. Add the onions and garlic, and sauté for 6 to 7 minutes until soft, making sure the onions and garlic do not turn brown. Combine the flour and milk, and whisk until very smooth. Add to the onions and garlic, bring to a simmer, and cook for 2 minutes. Season with salt and pepper. Whisk in the cheese, and fold in the cauliflower. Garnish with parsley.

125

Calories 90
Calories from Fat 20

Total Fat 2.5 g
Saturated Fat 1.4 g
Trans Fat 0 g

Cholesterol 10 mg
Sodium 80 mg*
Potassium 320 mg

Total Carbohydrate 12 g
Dietary Fiber 2 g
Sugars 6 g

Protein 6 g
Phosphorus 115 mg

*without added salt

MINTED BARLEY SALAD

2 teaspoons olive oil

1/2 small onion, minced

1 cup pearl barley

4 cups water

1 strip fresh lemon zest

2 medium plum tomatoes, seeded and cubed

6 ounces sliced fresh spinach

3 scallions, thinly sliced

DRESSING

1 tablespoon red wine vinegar

2 sun-dried tomatoes (not packed in oil), rehydrated and finely chopped

1 garlic clove, minced

1 1/2 tablespoons fresh minced mint

3 tablespoons olive oil

Sea salt and freshly ground black pepper to taste

GARNISH

Fresh mint sprig

1 Heat the oil in a large saucepan over medium heat. Add the onion, and sauté for 2 minutes. Add the barley, and sauté for 2 minutes. Add in the water and lemon zest, and bring to a boil. Lower the heat, cover, and simmer for about 40 minutes or until the barley is tender. Drain the excess water from the barley, remove the lemon zest, and discard. Add the barley to a salad bowl.

2 Add the plum tomatoes, spinach, and scallions to the barley.

3 To prepare the dressing, whisk together the red wine vinegar, sun-dried tomatoes, garlic, and fresh mint. In a thin stream, slowly add the olive oil, and whisk until the dressing is emulsified. Season the dressing with salt and pepper. Pour the dressing over the barley salad, and garnish with fresh mint.

127

Calories 140	Total Fat 7 g	Cholesterol 0 mg	Total Carbohydrate 19 g	Protein 2 g
Calories from Fat 65	Saturated Fat 0.9 g	Sodium 45 mg*	Dietary Fiber 3 g	Phosphorus 55 mg
	Trans Fat 0 g	Potassium 285 mg	Sugars 2 g	

*without added salt

CLASSIC POTATOES AU GRATIN

SAUCE

- 1 1/2 tablespoons nonhydrogenated butter-type tub spread (such as Smart Balance)
- 1 1/2 tablespoons all-purpose flour
  Salt and pepper to taste
- 1 2/3 cups 1% milk
- 1 1/2 cups shredded 75% reduced-fat cheddar cheese (extra sharp if available)

- 6 medium russet potatoes (about 6 ounces each), peeled and cut into 1-inch-thick slices

1 Preheat the oven to 375°F. To prepare the cheese sauce: Melt the buttery spread in a medium saucepan over medium heat. Add in the flour, salt, and pepper, and stir constantly with a wire whisk for 1 minute. Stir in the milk, and cook until thickened, stirring constantly. Stir in all the cheese, and cook for 30 seconds.

2 Place half of the potato slices in a 9×13-inch baking pan coated with cooking spray. Pour in half the cheese sauce. Add remaining potatoes in a layer, and pour in the remaining cheese sauce.

3 Cover the dish with foil, and bake for 1 to 1 1/2 hours or until potatoes are tender. Remove the foil, and broil the top of the casserole for 1 to 2 minutes if desired.

Calories 115	Total Fat 3 g	Cholesterol 5 mg	Total Carbohydrate 16 g	Protein 7 g
Calories from Fat 25	Saturated Fat 1.3 g	Sodium 130 mg*	Dietary Fiber 1 g	Phosphorus 125 mg
	Trans Fat 0 g	Potassium 285 mg	Sugars 2 g	

*without added salt

SIDES

SAFFRON BROWN RICE PILAF WITH PINE NUTS AND CHERRIES

2 teaspoons olive oil

1 medium onion, chopped

1 large carrot, peeled and diced

2 garlic cloves, minced

1 1/2 cups rinsed long-grain brown rice

Large pinch saffron threads

3 cups low-fat, reduced-sodium chicken broth

1/4 cup pine nuts

1/4 cup dried cherries

Salt and pepper to taste

1/4 cup fresh parsley, minced

1 Heat the oil in a large skillet over medium heat. Add the onion and carrot, and sauté for about 5 to 6 minutes. Add the garlic, and sauté for 2 minutes. Add in the dry brown rice, and sauté for 3 minutes.

2 Crumble the saffron threads into the chicken broth, and add the mixture to the brown rice. Bring the rice to a boil. Lower the heat, cover, and simmer for 45 to 50 minutes or until tender.

3 Meanwhile, toast the pine nuts in a small dry skillet over medium heat. Shake the pan frequently until the nuts are light brown and fragrant.

4 Add the nuts and cherries to the brown rice and mix. Season the dish with salt and pepper, and garnish with fresh parsley.

131

Calories 160	Total Fat 4 g	Cholesterol 0 mg	Total Carbohydrate 28 g	Protein 4 g
Calories from Fat 35	Saturated Fat 0.5 g	Sodium 160 mg*	Dietary Fiber 2 g	Phosphorus 150 mg
	Trans Fat 0 g	Potassium 195 mg	Sugars 4 g	

*without added salt

SIDES

SAGE STUFFING

30 slices (1 ounce each) day-old, whole-grain bread, crusts removed, cut into small cubes

1 tablespoon olive oil

1 large onion, chopped

3 large celery stalks, chopped

1/3 cup coarsely chopped walnuts

1/2 bunch fresh sage, stems removed, coarsely chopped

3 cups hot low-fat, reduced-sodium chicken broth

1 egg, lightly beaten

1/2 cup dried cranberries or dried cherries, coarsely chopped

Kosher salt and fresh-ground black pepper to taste

Paprika

1 Preheat the oven to 375°F. Add the bread to a large bowl.

2 Heat the olive oil in a large skillet over medium heat. Add the onions and celery, and sauté for 3 minutes. Add the walnuts and sauté for 2 minutes. Add in the sage and cook for 1 minute.

3 Add the onion-sage mixture to the bread. Pour the hot chicken broth and egg over the onion-sage mixture, and mix well (until moist). Add in the cranberries or cherries. Season well with salt and pepper. Add the mixture to a large casserole dish, and sprinkle with paprika. Bake for about 40 to 45 minutes, or until the top is browned and crusty.

133

Calories 190	**Total Fat 6 g**	**Cholesterol 20 mg**	**Total Carbohydrate 28 g**	**Protein 8 g**
Calories from Fat 55	Saturated Fat 0.9 g	**Sodium 385 mg***	Dietary Fiber 5 g	**Phosphorus 140 mg**
	Trans Fat 0 g	**Potassium 255 mg**	Sugars 7 g	

*without added salt

RUSTIC MASHED POTATOES WITH OLIVE OIL AND GARLIC

2 pounds peeled and halved russet potatoes

14 peeled, whole garlic cloves

1/4 cup olive oil

1/3 cup grated fresh Parmesan cheese

Kosher salt and fresh-ground black pepper to taste

1 Bring a large pot of salted water to a boil. Add the potatoes and garlic, and bring again to a boil. Lower the heat, cover, and simmer on low for about 25 to 35 minutes, or until the potatoes are very tender.

2 Drain the potatoes, saving 1/2 cup of the cooking liquid. Add the potatoes back to the pot. Place a dish towel over the pan, and replace the cover. Let the potatoes dry steam for 5 minutes.

3 Slowly add the cooking liquid to the potatoes, mashing well. Add the olive oil, and continue to mash the potatoes to the desired consistency. Add in the Parmesan cheese, salt, and pepper.

Calories 125	Total Fat 6 g	Cholesterol 5 mg	Total Carbohydrate 16 g	Protein 3 g
Calories from Fat 55	Saturated Fat 1.3 g	Sodium 30 mg*	Dietary Fiber 1 g	Phosphorus 50 mg
	Trans Fat 0 g	Potassium 250 mg	Sugars 1 g	

*without added salt

KASHA WITH CARAMELIZED ONIONS AND CREMINI MUSHROOMS

ONIONS AND MUSHROOMS

- 1 tablespoon olive oil
- 2 large onions (about 10 ounces each), halved and thinly sliced
- 2 cups water, divided
- 1 tablespoon sugar
- 8 ounces cremini mushrooms, cleaned, stemmed, and thickly sliced
- Kosher salt and freshly ground black pepper to taste

KASHA

- 1 teaspoon olive oil
- 1 cup kasha (buckwheat groats)
- Kosher salt and freshly ground black pepper to taste
- 2 cups reduced-sodium, low-fat chicken broth

GARNISH

1/3 cup minced fresh parsley

1 To prepare the onions and mushrooms, heat 1 tablespoon of olive oil in a large skillet. Add in the onions, and sauté on medium heat for about 10 to 12 minutes, stirring occasionally, being careful not to let them burn. Add a cup of the water, and continue to cook until the water is evaporated, stirring occasionally. Add the other cup of water, and cook until it is evaporated.

2 Add the sugar, and continue to cook until the onions are very brown. Add in the mushrooms, and cook for 5 minutes, until they are tender. Season with salt and pepper. Set aside.

3 For the kasha, heat 1 teaspoon of olive oil in a saucepan over medium heat. Add the kasha, salt, and pepper, and sauté for 5 minutes. Add the broth, bring to a boil, lower the heat, cover, and cook for 10 minutes, until the kasha is tender.

4 Add the cooked kasha to the onion-mushroom mixture, and toss well. Taste and correct the seasoning if desired. Garnish with minced parsley.

Calories 160	Total Fat 3.5 g	Cholesterol 0 mg	Total Carbohydrate 28 g	Protein 5 g
Calories from Fat 30	Saturated Fat 0.6 g	Sodium 180 mg*	Dietary Fiber 4 g	Phosphorus 135 mg
	Trans Fat 0 g	Potassium 420 mg	Sugars 7 g	

*without added salt

SIDES

CAULIFLOWER WITH PANCETTA AND ONIONS

2 tablespoons olive oil, divided

3 ounces sliced pancetta (unsmoked bacon)

1 medium onion, thinly sliced

1 small cauliflower (about 1 1/4 pounds), trimmed and cut into florets (about 6 cups)

Kosher salt and freshly ground black pepper to taste

1 bay leaf

2 tablespoons water

1 tablespoon fresh lemon juice

1 Heat 1 tablespoon of the olive oil in a large heavy skillet over medium heat. Add the pancetta and cook until it is crisp. Remove the pancetta with a slotted spoon. Set aside. Add in the onions, and turn the heat to medium low. Sauté the onions for about 8 minutes. Add in the cauliflower, salt, pepper, and bay leaf.

2 Add in the water, cover, and raise the heat to medium. Cook for about 10 to 15 minutes, stirring occasionally until the cauliflower is tender and lightly browned. Remove and discard the bay leaf. Add the cauliflower to a serving bowl. Mix together the remaining olive oil and lemon juice, and add to the cauliflower, mixing well. Top with the crisp pancetta.

Calories 55	Total Fat 4.5 g	Cholesterol 5 mg	Total Carbohydrate 2 g	Protein 2 g
Calories from Fat 40	Saturated Fat 1.1 g	Sodium 140 mg*	Dietary Fiber 1 g	Phosphorus 45 mg
	Trans Fat 0 g	Potassium 110 mg	Sugars 1 g	

*without added salt

CHICKEN/POULTRY

SPICY BARBECUE CHICKEN

CHICKEN

- 2 teaspoons olive oil
- 4 (4-ounce) skinless, boneless chicken breasts
- 4 teaspoons Spicy Barbeque Rub

SPICY BARBECUE RUB

- 2 tablespoons onion powder
- 1 teaspoon garlic powder
- 1 teaspoon chili powder
- 2 teaspoons dried oregano
- 2 teaspoons dried thyme
- 2 teaspoons paprika
- 1 teaspoon cayenne
- 1 teaspoon cumin
- 2 teaspoons dry mustard
- 1/2 teaspoon salt

1 Preheat an outdoor grill with the rack set 6 inches from the heat source. Coat the rack with cooking spray. (Alternatively, preheat an oven broiler with the rack set 4 inches from the heat source. Coat the broiler pan with nonstick cooking spray.)

2 For Spicy Barbecue Rub: Combine all rub ingredients.

3 Rub each chicken breast with 1/2 teaspoon of the oil. Coat both sides with 1 teaspoon of the Spicy Barbecue Rub.

4 Grill or broil the chicken breasts for about 5 to 6 minutes per side until cooked through.

SPICY BARBECUE CHICKEN

Calories 155	**Total Fat 5 g**	**Cholesterol 65 mg**	**Total Carbohydrate 1 g**	**Protein 24 g**
Calories from Fat 45	Saturated Fat 1.1 g	**Sodium 125 mg**	Dietary Fiber 0 g	**Phosphorus 185 mg**
	Trans Fat 0 g	**Potassium 225 mg**	Sugars 0 g	

RUB ONLY

Calories 5	**Total Fat 0 g**	**Cholesterol 0 mg**	**Total Carbohydrate 1 g**	**Protein 0 g**
Calories from Fat 0	Saturated Fat 0 g	**Sodium 65 mg**	Dietary Fiber 0 g	**Phopshorus 5 mg**
	Trans Fat 0 g	**Potassium 25 mg**	Sugars 0 g	

GREEK FETA CHICKEN

- 4 ounces uncooked orzo
- 4 (4-ounce) skinless, boneless chicken breasts
- 2 teaspoons ground oregano
- 1/2 teaspoon salt
- 1/4 teaspoon fresh ground black pepper
- 1/8 teaspoon ground red pepper
- 1 tablespoon olive oil, divided
- 1 small red pepper, sliced into strips
- 1 small green pepper, sliced into strips
- 2 teaspoons bottled minced garlic
- 1 1/2 tablespoons fresh lemon juice
- 1 ounce crumbled feta cheese

1. Cook the orzo according to package directions (but without added salt or fat). While the orzo cooks, sprinkle the chicken breasts with oregano, salt, pepper, and ground red pepper.

2. Heat 2 teaspoons of the oil in a large nonstick skillet over medium-high heat. Add the chicken breasts and cook on both sides for about 4 to 5 minutes until no longer pink. Remove the chicken from the skillet.

3. Drain orzo and keep warm.

4. Lower the heat to medium and add remaining oil. Saute the peppers for 3 minutes. Add the garlic and saute for 1 minute more. Add the lemon juice and cook for 1 minute. Add back the chicken breasts to the skillet. Top with feta cheese, cover, and cook 1 minute until cheese slightly melts. Serve over cooked orzo.

143

Calories 290	Total Fat 8 g	Cholesterol 70 mg	Total Carbohydrate 24 g	Protein 29 g
Calories from Fat 70	Saturated Fat 2.4 g	Sodium 430 mg	Dietary Fiber 2 g	Phosphorus 255 mg
	Trans Fat 0.1 g	Potassium 345 mg	Sugars 4 g	

JAMAICAN CHICKEN THIGHS

RUB

- 1 tablespoon garlic powder
- 2 teaspoons onion powder
- 2 teaspoons allspice
- 1 teaspoon thyme
- 1 teaspoon ginger
- 1/2 teaspoon nutmeg
- 1/4 teaspoon cayenne pepper
- 1/4 teaspoon salt
- 1/8 teaspoon black pepper

CHICKEN

- 6 boneless, skinless chicken thighs (about 1 pound)
- 2 teaspoons canola oil

1 Combine the rub ingredients together in a small bowl.

2 Rub the spice mixture over each chicken thigh.

3 Heat the oil in a large nonstick skillet over medium heat. Add the chicken thighs and cook on each side for 5 to 7 minutes until cooked through.

145

Calories 135	**Total Fat 7 g**	**Cholesterol 50 mg**	**Total Carbohydrate 3 g**	**Protein 14 g**
Calories from Fat 65	Saturated Fat 1.8 g	**Sodium 145 mg**	Dietary Fiber 1 g	**Phosphorus 105 mg**
	Trans Fat 0 g	**Potassium 160 mg**	Sugars 1 g	

MARINATED CHICKEN ENCHILADAS WITH BLACK BEANS

1 pound boneless, skinless chicken breasts, cut into cubes

1 teaspoon olive oil

Juice of 1 lime

1 teaspoon chili powder

2 scallions, minced

Salt and pepper to taste

1 teaspoon olive oil

1 (15-ounce) can black beans, drained and rinsed

6 (6-inch) whole-wheat tortillas

2/3 cup reduced-fat shredded Mexican cheese blend or Monterey Jack cheese, divided

Cooking spray

1 1/2 cups canned enchilada sauce

1 In a medium bowl, combine the chicken with the olive oil, lime juice, chili powder, scallions, salt, and pepper. Cover and marinate in the refrigerator for at least 1 hour and up to 24 hours.

2 Preheat the oven to 375°F. Remove the chicken from the marinade and discard any excess. Heat the olive oil in a nonstick skillet over medium heat. Add the chicken and sauté for 7 to 8 minutes until chicken is cooked through. Remove the chicken to a bowl and add the black beans.

3 Divide the chicken-and-bean filling among six tortillas. Top each with 1 tablespoon of the cheese. Roll up each tortilla and place seam-side down in a baking dish coated with cooking spray. Pour the sauce over the enchiladas and bake, covered, for about 20 minutes. Add the remaining cheese and bake, uncovered, for 5 minutes until cheese melts.

Calories 305	Total Fat 9 g	Cholesterol 55 mg	Total Carbohydrate 30 g	Protein 26 g
Calories from Fat 80	Saturated Fat 2.4 g	Sodium 585 mg*	Dietary Fiber 6 g	Phosphorus 295 mg
	Trans Fat 0 g	Potassium 580 mg	Sugars 4 g	

*without added salt

SPICED TURKEY BURGERS WITH DILL SAUCE

BURGERS

1 1/4 pounds ground turkey
    breast

1/4 cup seasoned bread
    crumbs

1 egg, beaten

1/4 cup minced parsley

1/4 cup finely minced onion

2 teaspoons light soy sauce

1 teaspoon Worcestershire
    sauce

1/2 teaspoon ground cumin

1/2 teaspoon paprika

Fresh-ground black
    pepper

1 teaspoon olive oil

SAUCE

1/2 cup plain, nonfat Greek-
    style yogurt

2 teaspoons finely minced dill

1 teaspoon apple cider
    vinegar

1/2 teaspoon grated lemon zest

Salt and pepper to taste

4 whole wheat hamburger
    buns, toasted (optional)*

Lettuce and tomato
    (optional)*

*Not included in nutritional
analysis.*

1 Combine all ingredients for the burgers and form into patties. Be sure to handle the meat lightly.

2 Heat a medium-sized skillet over medium heat. Add the olive oil and then the turkey burgers. Cook for about 5 to 7 minutes per side until the turkey is cooked through (an internal temperature reading should be 180°F). You may also cook these on an outdoor grill, coated with cooking spray. If grilling, cook on medium heat, grilling the patties for about 5 to 7 minutes per side.

3 Combine the ingredients for the yogurt sauce. Top the turkey burgers (with or without the buns) with the yogurt sauce. Serve with lettuce and tomato, if desired.

149

Calories 235
Calories from Fat 45

Total Fat 5 g
Saturated Fat 1.3 g
Trans Fat 0 g

Cholesterol 125 mg
Sodium 360 mg*
Potassium 580 mg

Total Carbohydrate 9 g
Dietary Fiber 1 g
Sugars 3 g

Protein 39 g
Phosphorus 425 mg

without added salt

CHICKEN/POULTRY

CORNISH GAME HENS À L'ORANGE

HENS

3 tablespoons minced fresh thyme

Salt and pepper to taste

3 small Cornish hens (about 1 pound each)

SAUCE

1 1/2 cups fresh orange juice

2 tablespoons sherry vinegar

1 tablespoon sugar

1 teaspoon cornstarch

1 tablespoon water

2 teaspoons butter

1 tablespoon Dijon mustard

2 teaspoons minced fresh thyme

1 tablespoon fresh orange zest

Salt and pepper to taste

3 small oranges, skin and pith cut off, sliced in 1/4-inch-thick half-moon

1 Preheat the oven to 500°F. Combine the thyme, salt, and pepper. With your fingers, lift up the skin of each hen. Slide the thyme, salt, and pepper mixture underneath the skin. Sprinkle some inside the cavity of the hen as well.

2 Coat a roasting rack with cooking spray. Place the rack inside a large roasting pan. Place the hens breast side down on the rack. Roast uncovered for about 15 minutes. Lower the heat to 400°F and continue to roast the hens until they are cooked through, about 25 to 30 minutes. Test by making sure the juices run clear and the legs move easily. Remove the hens from the oven, and tent with foil to keep warm.

3 To prepare the orange sauce, bring the orange juice, vinegar, and sugar to a simmer over medium heat. Whisk together the cornstarch and water. Slowly whisk it into the juice-vinegar mixture, bring to a boil while whisking, and continue to cook until sauce thickens. Remove from heat and whisk in the butter, mustard, thyme, and orange zest. Season to taste with salt and pepper.

4 To serve, cut each hen in half. Serve the hens skinless with the orange sauce and slices.

151

Calories 205	Total Fat 5 g	Cholesterol 105 mg	Total Carbohydrate 15 g	Protein 23 g
Calories from Fat 45	Saturated Fat 1.8 g	Sodium 130 mg*	Dietary Fiber 1 g	Phosphorus 165 mg
	Trans Fat 0 g	Potassium 460 mg	Sugars 13 g	

*without added salt

PECAN-CRUSTED CHICKEN

MARINADE

- 1/2 cup Dijon mustard
- 2 tablespoons dry white wine
- Salt and pepper to taste
- 4 (4-ounce) boneless, skinless chicken breasts

COATING

- 1/2 cup crushed wheat crackers
- 1/3 cup finely chopped pecans
- 1/4 teaspoon dried basil
- Salt and pepper to taste
- 1 1/2 tablespoons olive oil

1 In a shallow bowl, whisk together the mustard, wine, salt, and pepper. Add the chicken breasts, and turn to coat. Cover, and refrigerate for 4 hours.

2 Preheat the oven to 450°F. Coat a baking sheet with cooking spray. Remove the chicken from the refrigerator, and allow it to come to room temperature. Combine the crackers, pecans, basil, salt, and pepper. Drizzle in the oil, and mix well. Place the crumb mixture on a plate.

3 Remove a chicken breast from the marinade without wiping off the marinade. Lightly coat the chicken with the crumb mixture. Place the chicken breast on a baking sheet coated with cooking spray. Repeat the same procedure with the remaining chicken breasts.

4 Roast the chicken for about 25 to 30 minutes until cooked through but still juicy.

153

Calories 310	**Total Fat 18 g**	**Cholesterol 65 mg**	**Total Carbohydrate 11 g**	**Protein 27 g**
Calories from Fat 160	Saturated Fat 2.6 g	**Sodium 510 mg***	Dietary Fiber 2 g	**Phosphorus 250 mg**
	Trans Fat 0 g	**Potassium 285 mg**	Sugars 2 g	

*without added salt

ORANGE HOISIN SAUCE

1/2 cup low-fat, reduced-sodium chicken broth

1/4 cup fresh orange juice

2 tablespoons prepared hoisin sauce

1 tablespoon light (lower sodium) soy sauce

1 teaspoon dark sesame oil

1 teaspoon sugar

1/4 teaspoon grated fresh orange zest

1 tablespoon arrowroot or cornstarch

SWEET AND SOUR SAUCE

1/2 cup unsweetened pineapple juice

2 tablespoons red wine vinegar

1 tablespoon sugar

1 teaspoon light (lower sodium) soy sauce

1 teaspoon peeled and grated fresh ginger

2 garlic cloves, finely minced

2 teaspoons arrowroot or cornstarch

1 Combine all ingredients except the arrowroot or cornstarch. Whisk until smooth. Add in the arrowroot or cornstarch, and whisk again. Prepare Stir-Fried Chicken with Red Peppers (page 155) and drizzle desired sauce over stir-fry.

154

ORANGE HOISIN SAUCE

Calories 15	Total Fat 0.5 g	Cholesterol 0 mg	Total Carbohydrate 2 g	Protein 0 g
Calories from Fat 0	Saturated Fat 0.1 g	Sodium 105 mg	Dietary Fiber 0 g	Phosphorus 5 mg
	Trans Fat 0 g	Potassium 25 mg	Sugars 2 g	

SWEET AND SOUR SAUCE

Calories 15	Total Fat 0 g	Cholesterol 0 mg	Total Carbohydrate 3 g	Protein 0 g
Calories from Fat 0	Saturated Fat 0 g	Sodium 15 mg	Dietary Fiber 0 g	Phosphorus 0 mg
	Trans Fat 0 g	Potassium 20 mg	Sugars 2 g	

CHICKEN/POULTRY

STIR-FRIED CHICKEN WITH RED PEPPERS AND BROCCOLI

CHICKEN

- 1 pound boneless, skinless chicken breasts, cut into 1-inch-long, 1/2-inch-wide strips
- 1 tablespoon light (lower sodium) soy sauce
- 1 tablespoon rice vinegar
- 2 teaspoons arrowroot or cornstarch
- 1 tablespoon peanut or vegetable oil

AROMATICS

- 1 teaspoon peanut or vegetable oil
- 1 teaspoon peeled and grated fresh ginger
- 3 garlic cloves, minced

VEGETABLES

- 1 medium red bell pepper, cored and sliced
- 2 celery stalks, thinly sliced
- 2 cups broccoli florets
- 1/4 cup low-fat, reduced-sodium chicken broth
- 1 recipe of either Orange Hoisin Sauce or Sweet and Sour Sauce (page 154)

GARNISH

- 1/4 cup toasted almond slivers or cashews

1 Prepare the chicken: Mix the chicken strips, soy sauce, rice vinegar, and arrowroot or cornstarch in a medium bowl. Set aside to marinate for 15 minutes.

2 Heat a wok over high heat. Add the 1 tablespoon of peanut or vegetable oil, and stir-fry the chicken for about 4 to 5 minutes. Remove the chicken from the wok and set aside.

3 Prepare the aromatics: Add the 1 teaspoon of peanut or vegetable oil to the wok. Add in the ginger and garlic, and stir-fry for 30 seconds.

4 Add the red bell pepper strips and sliced celery. Stir-fry for 1 minute. Add in the broccoli, and stir-fry for 1 minute. Add in the chicken broth, cover, and steam for 3 minutes or until broccoli turns bright green and is crisp.

5 Add in the desired sauce, and cook for 1 minute or until the sauce thickens. Return the chicken to the wok, coating it with the sauce. Garnish with either almonds or cashews.

155

Calories 195	Total Fat 8 g	Cholesterol 45 mg	Total Carbohydrate 11 g	Protein 19 g
Calories from Fat 70	Saturated Fat 1.5 g	Sodium 385 mg	Dietary Fiber 2 g	Phosphorus 180 mg
	Trans Fat 0 g	Potassium 400 mg	Sugars 6 g	

ITALIAN CHICKEN WITH OLIVES AND CAPERS

1 tablespoon olive oil

4 (4-ounce) boneless, skinless chicken breasts

Kosher salt and freshly ground black pepper to taste

1/3 cup dry white wine

1 medium onion, chopped

2 garlic cloves, minced

1 (28-ounce) can whole plum tomatoes*

2 teaspoons dried basil

1 teaspoon dried oregano

Pinch sugar

Pinch dried red chili flakes

4 teaspoons drained capers

1/3 cup coarsely chopped black olives

1 tablespoon balsamic vinegar

1/2 cup fresh parsley, minced

*This recipe does not meet ADA guidelines for sodium (maximum 600 mg). You might try lowering the sodium by using the no-salt-added variety of canned plum tomatoes.

1 Heat the oil in a large skillet over medium-high heat. Sprinkle both sides of the chicken breasts with salt and pepper.

2 Add the chicken to the skillet, and sauté on both sides for 5 to 6 minutes per side, until cooked through. Remove the chicken from the skillet. Add the wine to the pan, and cook over medium-high heat until the wine is reduced by half, about 3 minutes, while scraping the brown bits from the bottom of the pan. Add in the onions, and sauté for 6 to 8 minutes. Add in the garlic, and sauté for 1 minute.

3 Add the tomatoes with their juice to a large bowl. Crush the tomatoes coarsely with your hands. Add the tomatoes and juice to the pan. Add in the basil and oregano. Raise the heat to high, and cook for 4 minutes. Lower the heat to medium, and add the sugar and dried red chili flakes. Cook over medium heat uncovered for 20 minutes, or until thick. Stir in the capers, olives, and reserved chicken. Cook on medium low for 5 minutes. Add in the vinegar, and garnish with fresh parsley.

Calories 245	Total Fat 8 g	Cholesterol 65 mg	Total Carbohydrate 16 g	Protein 27 g
Calories from Fat 70	Saturated Fat 1.5 g	Sodium 800 mg*	Dietary Fiber 3 g	Phosphorus 235 mg
	Trans Fat 0 g	Potassium 695 mg	Sugars 7 g	

*without added salt

CHICKEN NUGGETS

1 pound boneless, skinless chicken breasts

1 cup low-fat buttermilk

1 1/2 cups panko bread crumbs

2 teaspoons cayenne pepper

1 teaspoon garlic powder

1/4 teaspoon salt

Freshly ground black pepper

Olive oil cooking spray

1 Add the chicken to a large plastic bag. With a rolling pin or meat mallet, pound each chicken breast, one at a time, until thin. Cut all the chicken into a total of 20 pieces. Add the chicken to another large plastic bag, and add the buttermilk. Seal the bag, and marinate the chicken in the refrigerator overnight.

2 The next day, preheat the oven to 400°F. Line a baking sheet with parchment paper, or with foil that has been coated with cooking spray. On a plate, combine the panko bread crumbs with the cayenne pepper, garlic powder, salt, and pepper. Shake the excess buttermilk off each piece of chicken, and roll the chicken in the bread-crumb mixture, coating it well. You will not use all the bread crumbs.

3 Place the chicken nuggets in a single layer on the baking sheet, and coat the top of the nuggets with the olive oil cooking spray.

4 Bake the nuggets for about 10 minutes, or until golden brown. Serve with your own favorite lower-sodium dipping sauce.*

Nutritional analysis does not include optional dipping sauce.

159

Calories 185	Total Fat 3.5 g	Cholesterol 65 mg	Total Carbohydrate 11 g	Protein 26 g
Calories from Fat 30	Saturated Fat 1 g	Sodium 175 mg	Dietary Fiber 0 g	Phosphorus 220 mg
	Trans Fat 0 g	Potassium 270 mg	Sugars 2 g	

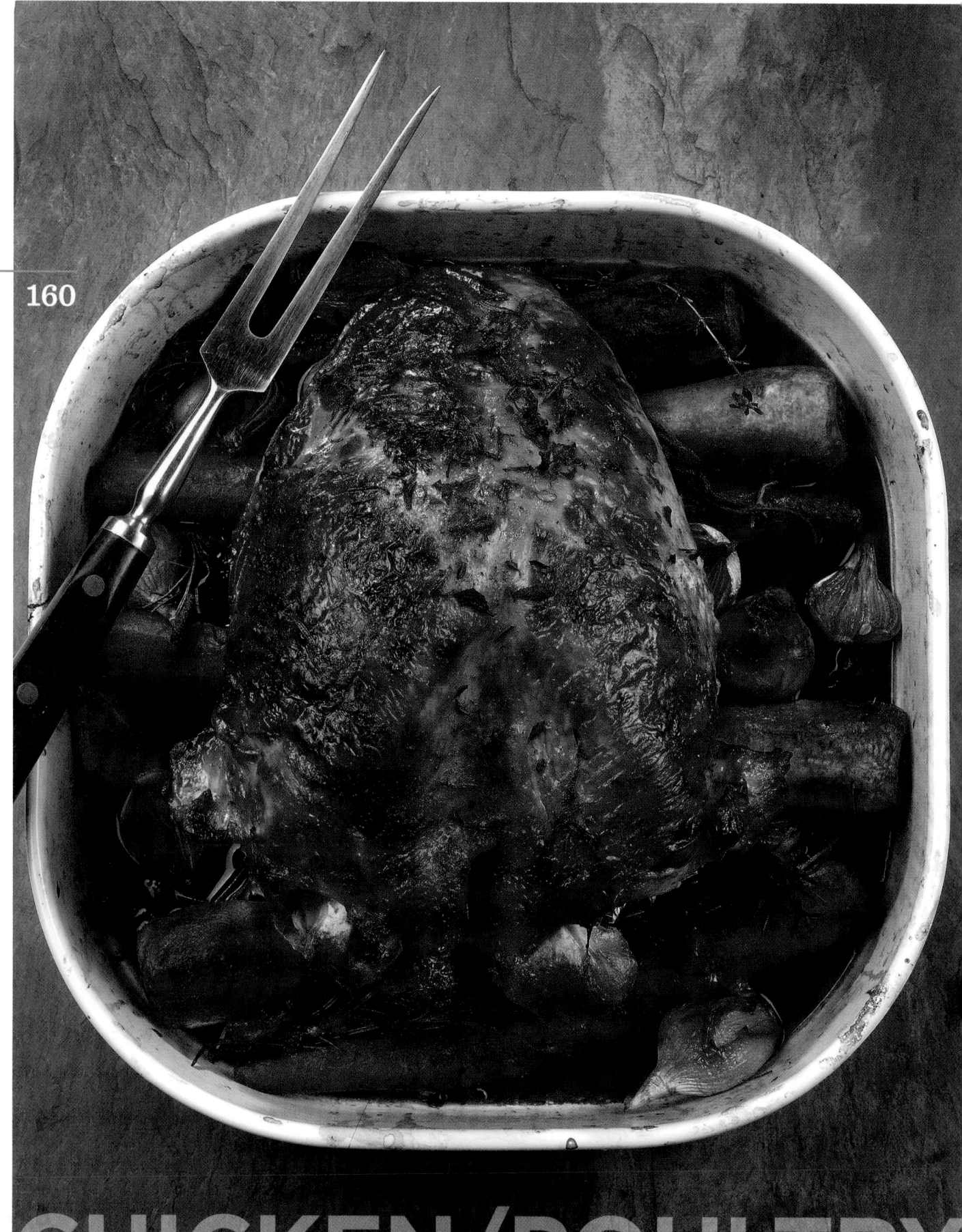

HERB-ROASTED TURKEY

5 teaspoons unsalted butter, softened

3 teaspoons fresh minced sage, divided

3 teaspoons fresh minced thyme, divided

3 teaspoons fresh minced rosemary, divided

Kosher salt and freshly ground black pepper to taste

1 1/2 cups low-fat, reduced-sodium chicken broth

1 cup dry white wine

1 (5-pound) turkey breast, skin on, washed and patted dry

1 Preheat the oven to 350°F. Line a large roasting pan with foil. Set a rack inside the roasting pan and coat it with cooking spray. Set aside.

2 In a small bowl, combine the butter with 2 teaspoons each of the sage, thyme, and rosemary, plus salt and pepper. Reserve the remaining 1 teaspoon of each of the herbs.

3 In a small saucepan, combine the chicken broth and wine, and bring to a gentle boil. Add the reserved herbs and lower to a simmer.

4 With your hands, separate the turkey breast skin from the breast meat, creating a pocket without removing the skin. Rub the butter-herb mixture all over the breast meat. Place the skin back down on the breast.

5 Set the turkey on the prepared rack in the pan. (You can also add veggies like peeled carrots, peeled parsnips, onions, or small potatoes to the pan; they will cook along with the turkey.) Roast the turkey for about 1 hour, 20 minutes to 1 hour, 40 minutes until the internal temperature reaches 170°F and the juices run clear. Baste every 15 to 20 minutes with the mixture of chicken broth and white wine.

6 Remove the turkey from the oven, cover loosely with foil, and let stand for 15 minutes before slicing. Discard the skin and serve.

Calories 165	Total Fat 2.5 g	Cholesterol 95 mg	Total Carbohydrate 0 g	Protein 33 g
Calories from Fat 20	Saturated Fat 1.4 g	Sodium 75 mg*	Dietary Fiber 0 g	Phosphorus 250 mg
	Trans Fat 0 g	Potassium 330 mg	Sugars 0 g	

*without added salt

HERB-ROASTED SALMON

4 (4-ounce) salmon filets

2 teaspoons olive oil

4 teaspoons All-Purpose Blend

ALL-PURPOSE BLEND

1/4 cup dried basil leaves

2 tablespoons crushed dried rosemary leaves

2 tablespoons dried marjoram leaves

2 tablespoons garlic powder

2 tablespoons dried thyme leaves

4 bay leaves, crushed

2 teaspoons dried sage leaves

2 teaspoons onion powder

1/2 teaspoon cayenne

1 Preheat the oven to 400°F. Rub each salmon filet with 1/2 teaspoon olive oil.

2 For the All-Purpose Blend: Combine all ingredients. Coat both sides of the salmon with 1 teaspoon of the All-Purpose Blend.

3 Add the salmon filets to a baking sheet.

4 Roast the salmon for about 8 to 9 minutes or until cooked through to your liking.

HERB-ROASTED SALMON

Calories 215	Total Fat 12 g	Cholesterol 75 mg	Total Carbohydrate 1 g	Protein 24 g
Calories from Fat 110	Saturated Fat 2 g	Sodium 60 mg	Dietary Fiber 0 g	Phosphorus 260 mg
	Trans Fat 0 g	Potassium 365 mg	Sugars 0 g	

ALL-PURPOSE BLEND ONLY

Calories 5	Total Fat 0 g	Cholesterol 0 mg	Total Carbohydrate 1 g	Protein 0 g
Calories from Fat 0	Saturated Fat 0 g	Sodium 0 mg	Dietary Fiber 0 g	Phosphorus 5 mg
	Trans Fat 0 g	Potassium 20 mg	Sugars 0 g	

TILAPIA TACOS

FISH

- 1 pound tilapia or other similar white fish filets
- 2 tablespoons fresh lime juice
- 2 teaspoons olive oil
- 1/2 teaspoon chili powder
- 2 garlic cloves, minced

SAUCE

- 1 cup plain, nonfat yogurt (preferably Greek-style)
- 1 1/2 tablespoons nonfat mayonnaise
- 2 tablespoons mild or hot salsa
- 2 teaspoons lime juice
- Fresh ground pepper to taste*

VEGETABLES

- 1 cup shredded green or red cabbage
- 1 large tomato, seeded and diced
- 1/3 cup minced cilantro
- 4 (8-inch) whole-wheat tortillas

GARNISH

- 4 thin slices fresh avocado
  *Not included in nutritional analysis.

1 To prepare the fish: Combine the fish with the lime juice, olive oil, chili powder, and garlic in a bowl, and let marinate for 30 minutes to 1 hour, covered, in the refrigerator.

2 Meanwhile, combine all the ingredients for the sauce and set aside.

3 Prepare the vegetables; set aside.

4 Remove the fish from the refrigerator, and heat the oven to broil. Cover a broiler pan with foil, and coat with cooking spray. Broil the fish for about 4 to 5 minutes per side until fish is cooked through. Remove from oven. Let fish cool slightly; flake into large pieces.

5 Heat each tortilla in a large skillet over medium heat, cooking the tortilla on each side for about 2 minutes until lightly browned.

6 Spread the inside of each tortilla with about 1 tablespoon of the sauce. Divide the fish among the tortillas and top with some of the vegetables. Fold over the tortilla to form a taco and garnish with a slice of avocado. Drizzle additional sauce over each taco.

Calories 345	Total Fat 8 g	Cholesterol 75 mg	Total Carbohydrate 34 g	Protein 33 g
Calories from Fat 70	Saturated Fat 2.1 g	Sodium 500 mg	Dietary Fiber 4 g	Phosphorus 360 mg
	Trans Fat 0 g	Potassium 785 mg	Sugars 8 g	

OVEN-ROASTED SALMON WITH LATIN SPICES AND SALSA

TROPICAL SALSA

2 small ripe mangoes (11 ounces each) or 1 large papaya, peeled and diced

1 cup diced fresh pineapple

1/2 small red onion, diced

1/4 cup minced cilantro or parsley

3 tablespoons fresh lime juice

1 teaspoon sugar

Salt to taste

RUB

1 tablespoon cumin

1 tablespoon coriander

2 teaspoons chili powder

1 tablespoon brown sugar

1 teaspoon kosher salt

1 teaspoon cinnamon

1/2 teaspoon cayenne pepper

1 teaspoon fresh ground pepper

1 1/2 pounds salmon filets

1 Combine all salsa ingredients in a bowl, cover, and refrigerate for 30 minutes.

2 Preheat oven to 400°F. Combine all rub ingredients and spread over both sides of the salmon. You may have leftover rub.

3 Line a broiler pan or baking sheet with foil and coat with cooking spray; place the salmon filets on the pan. Roast the salmon for about 10 minutes. Turn the oven to broil. Broil for 2 minutes to give the salmon a golden color. Serve with a side of the salsa.

Calories 270	Total Fat 10 g	Cholesterol 75 mg	Total Carbohydrate 20 g	Protein 25 g
Calories from Fat 90	Saturated Fat 1.8 g	Sodium 310 mg*	Dietary Fiber 2 g	Phosphorus 275 mg
	Trans fat 0 g	Potassium 540 mg	Sugars 16 g	

*without added salt

SPICY FISH WITH TAMARIND SAUCE

1 teaspoon black or yellow mustard seeds

1–2 dried red chilies

2 tablespoons tamarind paste

1/2 cup warm water

1 tablespoon olive oil

2 medium onions, sliced

2 cloves garlic, minced

2 teaspoons grated fresh ginger

2 teaspoons curry powder

Salt to taste

1 pound thick fish filets such as salmon, halibut, or cod, cut into 4 pieces

1 Grind the mustard seeds and chilies in a spice or coffee grinder. Set aside.

2 In a small bowl, mash together the tamarind paste and warm water until the water is very brown. Strain in a fine sieve, pressing out any solids. Discard the solids; retain the liquid. Set aside.

3 Heat the oil in a large skillet over medium heat. Add the onion and garlic and sauté for 5 minutes. Add the ginger and sauté for 2 minutes. Add the curry powder and mustard-chili mixture. Sauté for 1 minute. Add the tamarind water and a dash of salt. Add the fish filets, nestling them into the onion mixture. Cover, lower heat to a simmer, and cook for 10 minutes or until the fish is cooked through. Serve the fish with the sauce.

Calories 275	**Total Fat 14 g**	**Cholesterol 75 mg**	**Total Carbohydrate 12 g**	**Protein 26 g**
Calories from Fat 125	Saturated Fat 2.2 g	**Sodium 65 mg***	Dietary Fiber 2 g	**Phosphorus 295 mg**
	Trans Fat 0 g	**Potassium 530 mg**	Sugars 5 g	

*without added salt

MALAYSIAN SHRIMP WITH PINEAPPLE

2 teaspoons canola oil

1 onion, thinly sliced

3 garlic cloves, minced

1 teaspoon ground cumin

1 teaspoon turmeric

1 teaspoon ground coriander

1/8–1/4 teaspoon red pepper flakes

2 tablespoons lite soy sauce

1 tablespoon brown sugar

1/3 cup lite coconut milk

1 pound large shrimp, peeled and deveined

2 cups fresh pineapple chunks

2 scallions, thinly sliced

1 In a wok or a deep heavy pan, warm the oil over medium-high heat. Add the onions and garlic, and stir-fry for about 5 minutes until onions begin to soften. Add the cumin, turmeric, coriander, and red pepper flakes. Stir-fry for 2 minutes.

2 Combine the soy sauce, brown sugar, and coconut milk. Add to the wok, lower the heat, cover, and simmer for 5 minutes.

3 Add the shrimp into the sauce. Simmer uncovered for 3 to 4 minutes until shrimp are almost cooked through. Add the pineapple and scallions, and cook 1 minute.

Calories 195	Total Fat 4.5 g	Cholesterol 160 mg	Total Carbohydrate 21 g	Protein 19 g
Calories from Fat 40	Saturated Fat 1.1 g	Sodium 893 mg	Dietary Fiber 2 g	Phosphorus 250 mg
	Trans Fat 0 g	Potassium 370 mg	Sugars 14 g	

ZESTY SALMON BURGERS

2 teaspoons olive oil

1/2 cup finely chopped red onion

1/4 cup finely chopped celery

1 garlic clove, minced

1 pound skinned salmon filet, cut into 1-inch pieces

1 tablespoon Dijon mustard

1/4 cup panko bread crumbs

Dash Old Bay seasoning

SAUCE

1/4 cup nonfat mayonnaise

1 teaspoon small capers

1 teaspoon fresh lemon juice

1/4 teaspoon lemon zest

4 (1-ounce) whole-wheat hamburger buns (optional, not included in nutritional analysis)

4 thin tomato slices

4 lettuce leaves

1 Heat the olive oil in a skillet over medium heat. Add the red onion, celery, and garlic, and sauté for 3 minutes. Add the mixture to a bowl.

2 Add the salmon to a food processor, and pulse just until coarsely chopped. Add to the sautéed vegetables.

3 Add the mustard, bread crumbs, and Old Bay seasoning, and mix well. Shape into 4 (3/4-inch thick) patties.

4 Coat the rack of an outdoor grill with cooking spray. Bring the grill up to medium-high heat. Add the salmon patties, and cook for about 3 to 4 minutes per side.

5 Combine all the ingredients for the sauce.

6 Serve the salmon burgers (with or without the buns) with some of the sauce drizzled on top and a slice of tomato and lettuce. (Alternatively, sauce, tomato, and lettuce can be served alongside.)

173

Calories 265	**Total Fat 13 g**	**Cholesterol 80 mg**	**Total Carbohydrate 10 g**	**Protein 27 g**
Calories from Fat 115	Saturated Fat 2.1 g	**Sodium 310 mg**	Dietary Fiber 1 g	**Phosphorus 290 mg**
	Trans Fat 0 g	**Potassium 520 mg**	Sugars 3 g	

SIMPLE BAKED HALIBUT

4 (4-ounce) halibut steaks
8 sprigs fresh thyme
  Pinch of salt
  Pinch of ground pepper
4 coin-shaped lemon slices

1 Preheat oven to 375°F.

2 Put steaks in a baking dish; season with thyme, salt, and pepper. Place a lemon slice on top of each steak. Cover dish, place in the preheated oven, and bake until fish is firm and begins to flake in the thickest part. Remove from oven, and serve immediately.

Calories 130	Total Fat 2.5 g	Cholesterol 35 mg	Total Carbohydrate 2 g	Protein 24 g
Calories from Fat 20	Saturated Fat 0.4 g	Sodium 60 mg	Dietary Fiber 1 g	Phosphorus 255 mg
	Trans Fat 0 g	Potassium 535 mg	Sugars 0 g	

SHRIMP-STUFFED FLOUNDER

STUFFING MIXTURE

- 1/2 slice bacon, diced
- 1 small onion, diced
- 2 garlic cloves, minced
- 1/2 pound small cooked shrimp, peeled and deveined
- 1 (10-ounce) package frozen spinach, thawed, drained well, and patted dry
- Pinch nutmeg
- Kosher salt and fresh-ground black pepper to taste
- 1/3 cup nonfat sour cream
- 1/2 cup panko bread crumbs
- 1/4 cup freshly grated Parmesan cheese

- 4 (5-ounce) flounder filets
- 1 teaspoon olive oil
- Paprika

1. Preheat the oven to 350°F. Coat a 9-inch-square baking pan with cooking spray. Set aside.

2. Sauté the bacon over medium heat until cooked through and crispy. Remove the bacon from the pan, and set aside to cool.

3. Add the onion and garlic to the drippings in the pan, and sauté over medium heat for about 4 to 5 minutes. Add in the shrimp, and sauté for 2 to 3 minutes. Add in the spinach, nutmeg, salt, and pepper, and heat through for 1 to 2 minutes. Remove the pan from the heat.

4. Add the shrimp-and-spinach mixture to a large bowl. Add in the sour cream, bread crumbs, Parmesan cheese, and bacon crumbles.

5. Working on a flat surface, add a scoop of the stuffing to one end of a flounder filet. Roll the flounder over the stuffing, and secure with a toothpick. Repeat with the remaining filets.

6. Place the rolls in the prepared pan. Drizzle the top of each fish roll with olive oil. Sprinkle with paprika.

7. Bake the fish for about 20 to 25 minutes or until cooked through.

Calories 290	Total Fat 7 g	Cholesterol 150 mg	Total Carbohydrate 15 g	Protein 40 g
Calories from Fat 65	Saturated Fat 2.4 g	Sodium 600 mg*	Dietary Fiber 3 g	Phosphorus 515 mg
	Trans Fat 0 g	Potassium 685 mg	Sugars 3 g	

*without added salt

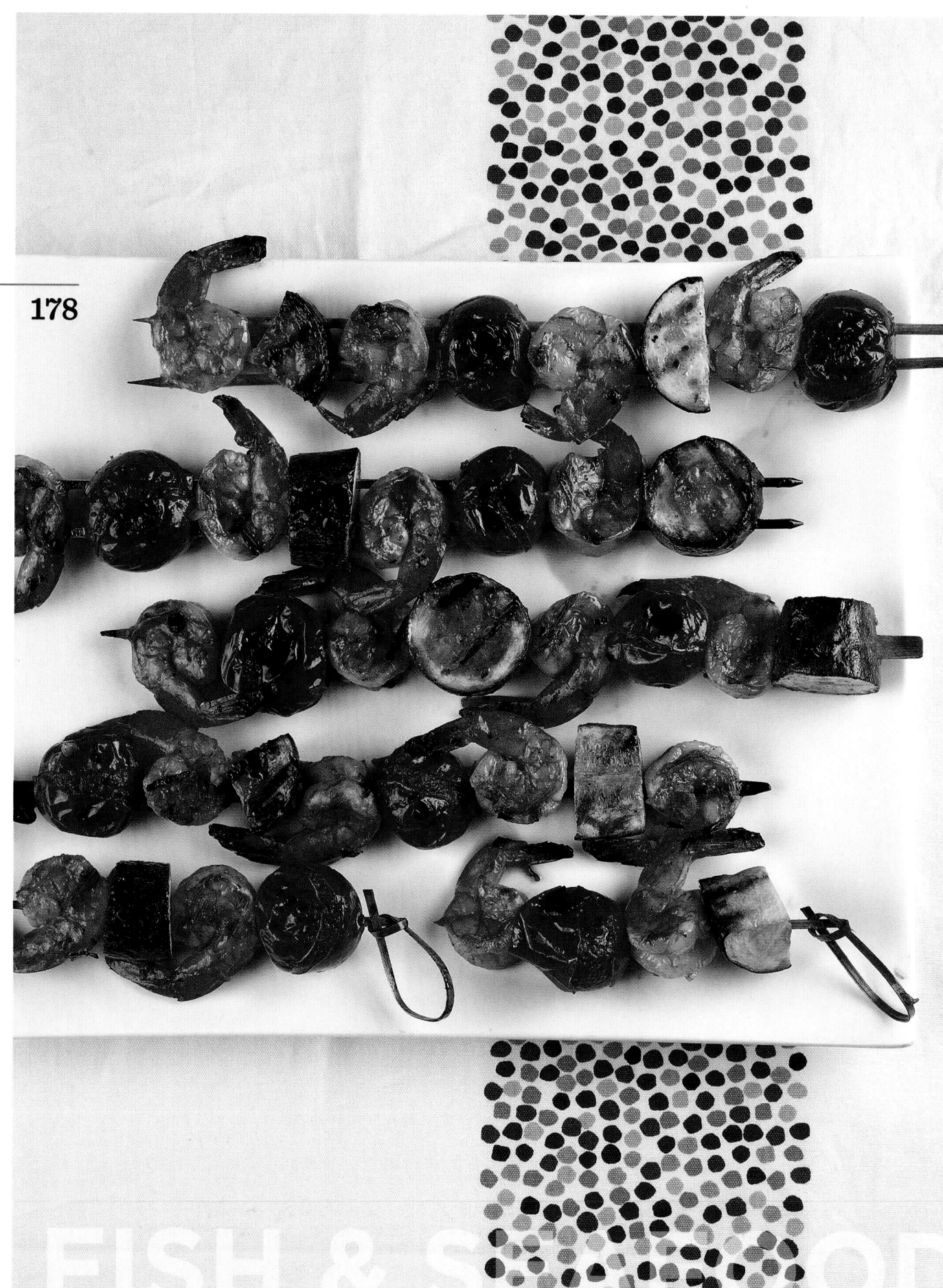

EXCHANGES with Lemon Garlic Marinade: 1 Vegetable, 3 Lean meat, 1 Fat
EXCHANGES with Asian Barbecue Sauce: 1/2 Carbohyhdrate, 1 Vegetable, 3 Lean meat

SHRIMP AND VEGETABLE KEBABS TWO WAYS

- 16 wooden skewers
- 1 pound large peeled and deveined shrimp (approximately 32 shrimp)
- 16 cherry tomatoes
- 1 unpeeled, medium zucchini, cut into 16 (3/4-inch) chunks

LEMON GARLIC MARINADE

- 1/4 cup fresh lemon juice
- 2 tablespoons olive oil
- Zest of 1 lemon
- 5 garlic cloves, minced

ASIAN BARBECUE SAUCE

- 1/4 cup hoisin sauce
- 2 tablespoons low-fat, reduced-sodium chicken broth
- 1 1/2 tablespoons lite soy sauce
- 1 tablespoon dry sherry
- 2 teaspoons brown sugar
- 1 teaspoon dark sesame oil
- 2 garlic cloves, minced

1. Soak the skewers in a pan of hot water for at least 30 minutes to prevent them from burning.

2. Prepare the grill: Coat the rack with cooking spray, or use tongs to dip a large piece of paper towel into vegetable oil and rub it on the grill rack. (Discard the towel.) Set the grill to medium-high on a gas grill, or prepare a medium-high fire on a charcoal grill.

3. For the Lemon Garlic Marinade: Combine all the marinade ingredients in a nonreactive bowl (e.g., glass, glaze-free ceramic, or stainless steel, not aluminum or unlined copper). Marinate the shrimp for 15 minutes at room temperature.

   For the Asian Barbecue Sauce: Combine all the ingredients in a small bowl. (Apply in step 5.)

4. For each kebab, hold two wooden skewers together, and thread on 4 shrimp, 2 cherry tomatoes, and 2 pieces of zucchini, alternating between a shrimp and a vegetable.

5. To grill: Place either choice of kebab on the rack. For the lemon garlic version, brush the shrimp with any excess marinade. For the Asian-style shrimp, begin by brushing on some of the sauce.

6. Grill the shrimp kebabs for about 4 minutes, turn, and cook the other side for another 4 minutes or until the shrimp is cooked through and the vegetables become softened. For the Asian-style shrimp, keep brushing on the sauce until it is used up.

7. Remove the kebabs from the grill and serve.

KABOBS WITH LEMON GARLIC MARINADE

Calories 200	Total Fat 8 g	Cholesterol 185 mg	Total Carbohydrate 6 g	Protein 26 g
Calories from Fat 70	Saturated Fat 1.3 g	Sodium 970 mg	Dietary Fiber 1 g	Phosphorus 205 mg
	Trans Fat 0 g	Potassium 510 mg	Sugars 3 g	

KABOBS WITH ASIAN BARBECUE SAUCE

Calories 190	Total Fat 3 g	Cholesterol 185 mg	Total Carbohydrate 12 g	Protein 27 g
Calories from Fat 25	Saturated Fat 0.6 g	Sodium 1380 mg	Dietary Fiber 1 g	Phosphorus 295 mg
	Trans Fat 0 g	Potassium 525 mg	Sugars 9 g	

ROASTED SEA BASS WITH WINE AND HERBS

1/4 cup olive oil, divided

1 1/2 pounds boneless sea bass filets or other firm white fish, such as cod

1/2 cup dry white wine

2 garlic cloves, minced

1 tablespoon fresh minced oregano or thyme

Pinch crushed red pepper flakes

Kosher salt and freshly ground black pepper to taste

1 Preheat the oven to 425°F. Coat a large baking pan with about 1 teaspoon of the olive oil. Arrange the fish filets in a single layer in the pan. Brush some of the olive oil over all the filets.

2 Combine the remaining olive oil, wine, garlic, oregano or thyme, red pepper flakes, salt, and pepper. Mix well. Pour over the fish filets.

3 Roast the fish for about 10 minutes, or until cooked through and opaque. Remove from the pan; pour pan juices over the fish. Drizzle with additional olive oil as desired.

Calories 200
Calories from Fat 100*

Total Fat 11 g
Saturated Fat 1.8 g
Trans Fat 0 g

Cholesterol 45 mg
Sodium 80 mg**
Potassium 305 mg

Total Carbohydrate 1 g
Dietary Fiber 0 g
Sugars 0 g

Protein 21 g
Phosphorus 225 mg

*without added olive oil
**without added salt

COD IN PARCHMENT

Parchment paper

1 (4-ounce) fresh cod filet, 3/4- to 1-inch thick

1 slice tomato, 1/4 inch thick

Kosher salt and freshly ground black pepper to taste

1/4 teaspoon dried oregano

1 teaspoon fresh lime juice

1/2 teaspoon olive oil

1 Preheat the oven or toaster oven to 400°F. Tear off a large piece of parchment paper. Fold the parchment in half. Using scissors, cut a half heart shape. Open the parchment. You should have a heart-shaped piece of paper.

2 Place the cod filet on one side of the heart. Lay the tomato slice over the cod. Sprinkle with salt, pepper, and dried oregano. Drizzle the lime juice and olive oil over the fish. Fold the parchment paper into a heart half again, and crimp the edges to seal (the pouch should look like an empanada). Place the packet on a baking sheet or a large toaster oven tray.

3 Bake the fish for about 10 to 12 minutes, or until it is cooked through. Remove the fish packet from the oven, carefully unseal the package, and transfer the fish and juices to a plate.

183

Calories 120	Total Fat 3 g	Cholesterol 50 mg	Total Carbohydrate 1 g	Protein 20 g
Calories from Fat 25	Saturated Fat 0.5 g	Sodium 70 mg*	Dietary Fiber 0 g	Phosphorus 130 mg
	Trans Fat 0 g	Potassium 270 mg	Sugars 1 g	

without added salt

SEARED SCALLOPS WITH CUCUMBER CHIVE MINT RELISH

MINT CHIVE RELISH

- 1 cup peeled, seeded, and diced cucumber (about 1 medium)
- 1/2 cup peeled, diced Gala apple
- 1/2 cup minced fresh chives
- 2 tablespoons minced fresh mint
- 2 tablespoons minced fresh cilantro
- 2 tablespoons fresh lime juice
- 1 teaspoon olive oil
- 1/2 teaspoon fresh lime zest
- 1/2 teaspoon sugar
- 1/8 teaspoon cayenne pepper
- 1/8 teaspoon salt
  Pinch freshly ground black pepper

- 2 tablespoons all-purpose flour
- 1 teaspoon ground cumin
- 1/8 teaspoon salt
  Freshly ground black pepper to taste
- 1 pound sea scallops
- 1 tablespoon canola oil
- 1 teaspoon unsalted butter

1 In a small serving bowl, combine all the ingredients for the relish, cover, and refrigerate. You should have about 2 cups of relish.

2 In a shallow bowl, combine the flour, ground cumin, salt, and black pepper, and mix well. Coat the scallops lightly with the flour mixture. Discard any leftover flour mixture.

3 Heat a heavy skillet, preferably cast iron, over medium-high heat. Add the canola oil and butter, and heat until small wisps of smoke are visible. Add the scallops, in batches if necessary to avoid crowding, and sear for 2 to 3 minutes on one side. Turn the scallops and sear for 2 minutes more or until they are cooked through and golden brown. Cook any large scallops a bit longer.

4 Serve the scallops with the relish.

185

Calories 180	Total Fat 7 g	Cholesterol 35 mg	Total Carbohydrate 12 g	Protein 19 g
Calories from Fat 65	Saturated Fat 1.3 g	Sodium 380 mg	Dietary Fiber 1 g	Phosphorus 385 mg
	Trans Fat 0 g	Potassium 385 mg	Sugars 3 g	

SERVING SIZE 4 ounces fish + 1/4 cup relish | **SERVES** 4
PREP/COOK TIME 15 minutes + marinating time/10 minutes
EXCHANGES 1/2 Fruit (relish), 3 Lean meat

TROPICAL TILAPIA WITH KIWI PINEAPPLE RELISH

4 tablespoons fresh lime juice

2 tablespoons olive oil

1 tablespoon finely minced fresh cilantro

1/4 teaspoon ground cumin

1/4 teaspoon ground coriander

1/8 teaspoon cayenne pepper

4 (4–5 ounces each) tilapia filets

Salt and freshly ground black pepper, optional

KIWI PINEAPPLE RELISH

3 medium kiwifruit, peeled and cut into 1/2-inch cubes

1/2 cup fresh diced pineapple

1 small red bell pepper, cored, seeded, and diced

2 scallions (white part only), minced

1/2 small jalapeño pepper, seeded and minced

1 tablespoon honey or brown sugar

1/4 teaspoon ground cumin

1 In a large bowl, combine the lime juice, olive oil, cilantro, cumin, coriander, and cayenne pepper. Add the tilapia, turning to coat. Cover and chill the tilapia for 30 minutes to 2 hours in the refrigerator.

2 For the Kiwi Pineapple Relish: In a small bowl, combine the ingredients, mixing well. Cover and refrigerate until serving time.

3 Remove the tilapia from the refrigerator, and allow it to come to room temperature for 15 minutes. Cover a broiler tray with foil, and coat it with cooking spray. Drain the marinade from the tilapia; if desired, season with salt and black pepper. Broil the tilapia about 6 inches from the heat source for 4 to 5 minutes per side or until the fish flakes easily with a fork.

4 Serve the tilapia with chilled Kiwi Pineapple Relish.

COOK'S TIP | Cover and refrigerate leftover relish; use within 3 days. This relish is tasty as a condiment for tilapia, grilled chicken, as a sandwich spread, and on fresh greens.

TROPICAL TILAPIA WITH KIWI PINEAPPLE RELISH

Calories 175	Total Fat 6 g	Cholesterol 50 mg	Total Carbohydrate 9 g	Protein 23 g
Calories from Fat 55	Saturated Fat 1.3 g	Sodium 50 mg*	Dietary Fiber 1 g	Phosphorus 190 mg
	Trans Fat 0 g	Potassium 480 mg	Sugars 6 g	
				*without added salt

KIWI PINEAPPLE RELISH ONLY

Calories 35	Total Fat 0 g	Cholesterol 0 g	Total Carbohydrate 9 g	Protein 1 g
Calories from Fat 0	Saturated Fat 0 g	Sodium 0 g	Dietary Fiber 1 g	Phosphorus 15 mg
	Trans Fat 0 g	Potassium 145 mg	Sugars 6 g	

SERVING SIZE 4 ounce filet + 2 tablespoons sauce | **SERVES** 4
PREP/COOK TIME 10 minutes/8 minutes + 2 hours to chill
EXCHANGES 4 Lean meat, Free food (sauce)

POACHED SALMON WITH SPICED YOGURT SAUCE

1/2 cup dry white wine

1/2 cup water

2 whole peppercorns

1 small onion, thinly sliced

1 sprig fresh parsley

1 sprig fresh dill

1 pound fresh salmon filet, skinned and cut into 4 pieces

SPICED YOGURT SAUCE

1 cup plain fat-free Greek-style yogurt

1/3 cup low-fat mayonnaise

1 tablespoon fresh lemon or lime juice

1/4 cup minced scallion (white part only)

1/4 cup minced cilantro

1 teaspoon ground cumin

1/4 teaspoon ground coriander

1/8 teaspoon cayenne pepper

Salt and freshly ground black pepper to taste (optional)

1 Add the wine, water, peppercorns, onion, parsley, and dill to a large skillet. Bring to a boil, and lower the heat to a simmer. Lay the salmon filets in the poaching liquid, cover, and simmer on low for 6 to 8 minutes. Do not overcook.

2 Remove the salmon carefully using a large slotted spatula. Discard the poaching liquid. Add the salmon to a covered container and refrigerate for 2 hours until cold.

3 For the Spiced Yogurt Sauce: Whisk all ingredients together.

4 Serve salmon with Spiced Yogurt Sauce, or flake the salmon for salads or sandwiches.

COOK'S TIP | Cover and refrigerate leftover yogurt sauce; use within 1 to 2 days.

POACHED SALMON ONLY

Calories 165	**Total Fat 7 g**	**Cholesterol 50 mg**	**Total Carbohydrate 0 g**	**Protein 24 g**
Calories from Fat 65	Saturated Fat 1.4 g	**Sodium 45 mg**	Dietary Fiber 0 g	**Phosphorus 265 mg**
	Trans Fat 0 g	**Potassium 405 mg**	Sugars 0 g	

SPICED YOGURT SAUCE ONLY

Calories 20	**Total Fat 0 g**	**Cholesterol 0 mg**	**Total Carbohydrate 2 g**	**Protein 2 g**
Calories from Fat 0	Saturated Fat 0 g	**Sodium 65 mg***	Dietary Fiber 0 g	**Phosphorus 35 mg**
	Trans Fat 0 g	**Potassium 65 mg**	Sugars 1 g	

*without added salt

PORK CHOPS STUFFED WITH APPLES AND DATES

2 tablespoons sweet Madeira wine, divided

2 cups chopped Gala apples, unpeeled

1/2 cup diced pitted dates

2 tablespoons coarsely chopped walnuts

2 tablespoons minced fresh thyme

1 teaspoon honey

8 (4-ounce) lean boneless pork chops (about 3/4–1 inch thick)

Salt and pepper to taste

2 teaspoons canola oil

1 Combine the wine with the apples, dates, walnuts, thyme, and honey.

2 Make a horizontal slit in each pork chop. Stuff equal portions of the mixture into each chop.

3 Sprinkle each chop with salt and pepper.

4 Heat a large skillet over medium heat. Add half the canola oil, and sear 4 of the chops for about 7 to 8 minutes per side. Add the remaining oil to the pan, and repeat with the remaining chops.

Calories 230	Total Fat 10 g	Cholesterol 60 mg	Total Carbohydrate 14 g	Protein 22 g
Calories from Fat 90	Saturated Fat 2.8 g	Sodium 45 mg*	Dietary Fiber 2 g	Phosphorus 190 mg
	Trans Fat 0 g	Potassium 410 mg	Sugars 12 g	

*without added salt

PORK/BEEF

SERVING SIZE 3 ounces meat + 3 tablespoons sauce | **SERVES** 14
PREP/COOK TIME 10 minutes/1 hour, 10 minutes + resting time
EXCHANGES 3 Lean meat

ROAST BEEF WITH CREAMY ✓ HORSERADISH SAUCE

ROAST BEEF

- 1 1/2 tablespoons cracked black pepper
- 2 teaspoons kosher salt
- 5 garlic cloves, finely minced
- 1 (3-pound) sirloin tip roast or bottom round roast, all excess fat removed (leave at room temperature for 15 minutes before roasting)

CREAMY HORSERADISH SAUCE

- 2 cups nonfat sour cream
- 1/2 cup peeled, grated fresh horseradish or prepared horseradish
- 1/4 cup coarse Dijon mustard

1 Preheat the oven to 450°F. Combine the black pepper, salt, and garlic, and rub all over the roast. Place the meat in a large roasting pan. Roast the meat for about 20 minutes.

2 Reduce the heat to 325°F, and bake for about 50 additional minutes or until a meat thermometer inserted in the roast registers 140°F for medium rare. Cook longer if desired.

3 Remove the roast from the oven. Cover loosely with foil, and let stand for 15 to 20 minutes. Cut the meat across the grain into thin slices.

4 Combine the ingredients for the horseradish sauce, and serve with the sliced beef.

Calories 170	Total Fat 4.5 g	Cholesterol 60 mg	Total Carbohydrate 4 g	Protein 25 g
Calories from Fat 40	Saturated Fat 1.5 g	Sodium 455 mg	Dietary Fiber 1 g	Phosphorus 190 mg
	Trans Fat 0 g	Potassium 275 mg	Sugars 2 g	

FILET MIGNON WITH RED WINE SHALLOT SAUCE

2 (4-ounce) filet mignons

Kosher salt and fresh-ground black pepper

2 teaspoons olive oil

SAUCE ✓

1 small shallot, finely minced

3 tablespoons dry red wine

1/2 cup fat-free, reduced-sodium beef broth

1 tablespoon Dijon mustard

3 tablespoons fat-free sour cream

Salt and pepper to taste

1 Sprinkle each filet on both sides with salt and pepper.

2 In a cast-iron skillet or similar heavy pan, heat the oil over high heat. When the oil is hot, add the steaks and sear on one side for about 5 minutes. If the filet starts to cook too quickly, lower the temperature to medium high. Turn the filet over, and continue to cook about 4 minutes. This will produce a rare filet. If desired, cook longer to your liking. Remove the filets from the skillet, and set aside to keep warm.

3 To make the sauce, add the shallots to the pan (if there are not enough pan drippings to cook the shallots, add just a bit of beef broth). Cook the shallots for 1 minute. Add in the wine, and cook until the wine almost evaporates. Add in the beef broth, and reduce until half its volume. Whisk in the mustard, and stir until smooth. Remove from the heat, and whisk in the sour cream until smooth. Season with salt and pepper. Serve each steak with about 2 tablespoons of sauce.

Calories 220	Total Fat 11 g	Cholesterol 60 mg	Total Carbohydrate 4 g	Protein 24 g
Calories from Fat 100	Saturated Fat 2.8 g	Sodium 345 mg*	Dietary Fiber 1 g	Phosphorus 205 mg
	Trans Fat 0 g	Potassium 375 mg	Sugars 1 g	

*without added salt

PORK/BEEF

PORK TENDERLOIN WITH APRICOT MUSTARD SAUCE

SAUCE

- 1/2 cup no-sugar-added apricot preserves
- 1/4 cup low-fat, reduced-sodium chicken broth
- 2 tablespoons coarse Dijon mustard
- 1 tablespoon light soy sauce
- 1/4 teaspoon ground cayenne pepper

PORK

- 2 teaspoons ground cumin
- 1 teaspoon ground coriander
- Kosher salt and freshly ground black pepper to taste
- 1 pound pork tenderloin, cut into 4 portions
- 2 teaspoons olive oil

1 Combine all the ingredients for the sauce and set aside.

2 Combine the cumin, coriander, salt, and pepper in a shallow bowl.

3 Coat both sides of the pork with the combined spices. Heat the oil in a large skillet over medium-high heat. Add the pork tenderloin, and sauté on both sides for about 6 minutes per side. Remove from the skillet and place on a plate. Slice into 1-inch-thick medallions (the meat will be rare in the middle). Set aside.

4 Add the sauce to the pan, and cook for 1 to 2 minutes, scraping up any browned bits from the pan. Add back the pork tenderloin with any accumulated juices, and cook for 1 to 2 minutes per side until fully cooked through.

Calories 230	Total Fat 6 g	Cholesterol 60 mg	Total Carbohydrate 22 g	Protein 23 g
Calories from Fat 55	Saturated Fat 1.3 g	Sodium 410 mg*	Dietary Fiber 1 g	Phosphorus 220 mg
	Trans Fat 0 g	Potassium 430 mg	Sugars 17 g	

*without added salt

PORK/BEEF

CHERRY-GLAZED PORK CHOP

1 teaspoon olive oil

1 (4-ounce) boneless pork loin chop

Kosher salt and freshly ground black pepper to taste

1/3 cup low-fat, reduced-sodium chicken broth

2 teaspoons balsamic vinegar

1 teaspoon brown sugar

1 tablespoon dried cherries, halved

1/2 teaspoon cornstarch

2 teaspoons water

1 Heat the olive oil in a small skillet over medium-high heat. Season the pork chop on both sides with salt and pepper, and sear on both sides for about 3 to 5 minutes per side, until cooked through. Remove from the skillet.

2 Combine the broth, vinegar, brown sugar, and dried cherries. Add to the pan, scraping up any browned bits. Simmer on medium-high heat for 1 minute.

3 Combine the cornstarch and water. Add to the cherry mixture and cook until thickened, about 30 seconds. Add back the pork chop and any accumulated juices. Simmer on low heat for 1 minute, flipping once to coat.

Calories 265	Total Fat 12 g	Cholesterol 60 mg	Total Carbohydrate 16 g	Protein 22 g
Calories from Fat 110	Saturated Fat 3.2 g	Sodium 220 mg*	Dietary Fiber 1 g	Phosphorus 240 mg
	Trans Fat 0 g	Potassium 395 mg	Sugars 13 g	

*without added salt

CAJUN-SPICED PORK TENDERLOIN

CAJUN RUB

- 1 tablespoon sweet paprika
- 1 teaspoon garlic powder
- 1 teaspoon onion powder
- 1/2 teaspoon dried thyme leaves
- 1 teaspoon dried oregano leaves
- 1/4 teaspoon cayenne pepper
  Freshly ground black pepper to taste

- 1 pound pork tenderloin, trimmed of excess fat
- 2 teaspoons olive oil

1 Preheat the oven to 400°F. Coat a roasting pan rack with cooking spray.

2 In a small bowl, combine all the ingredients for the Cajun Rub.

3 Rub the pork tenderloin with the olive oil. Coat both sides of the pork with the rub, making sure to use all of the rub. Roast the pork until the internal temperature reads 150–160°F, about 25 to 30 minutes. (If you prefer well-done pork, add cooking time to bring the internal temperature to 170°F.)

4 Remove the pork from the oven, and allow it to stand for 10 minutes before slicing.

COOK'S TIP | This pork works well on an open-faced sandwich, as pictured (with roasted red peppers and arugula).

Calories 120	Total Fat 4.5 g	Cholesterol 50 mg	Total Carbohydrate 2 g	Protein 18 g
Calories from Fat 40	Saturated Fat 1.1 g	**Sodium 35 mg**	Dietary Fiber 1 g	**Phosphorus 165 mg**
	Trans Fat 0 g	**Potassium 325 mg**	Sugars 0 g	

SERVING SIZE 2 1/2 ounce steak + 1 cup salad + 1 1/2 tablespoons dressing + 1 teaspoon seeds | **SERVES** 6
PREP/COOK TIME 10 minutes/16 minutes
EXCHANGES 1 Vegetable, 2 Lean meat, 1/2 Fat, Free food (dressing)

FLANK STEAK SALAD WITH CREAMY HERB DRESSING

CREAMY HERB DRESSING

- 1/4 cup chopped fresh dill
- 1/4 cup chopped fresh flat–leaf parsley
- 3 scallions, minced
- 2 tablespoons minced fresh thyme
- 3/4 cup fat-free mayonnaise
- 1/2 cup low-fat buttermilk
- 1 1/4 tablespoons red wine vinegar
- 1/4 teaspoon salt
- Dash hot sauce

Freshly ground black pepper to taste

1 pound flank steak

SALAD

- 4 cups mixed greens or torn romaine lettuce
- 1 small red pepper, thinly sliced
- 1/2 small red onion, very thinly sliced
- 1 cup quartered cherry tomatoes (about 1/2 pint)
- 1/4 cup sliced fresh basil (about 10 leaves)
- 2 tablespoons pumpkin seeds

(Continued on next page)

202

1. For the dressing, add the dill, parsley, scallions, thyme, and mayonnaise to a blender or food processor and process for 1 minute. With the motor running, slowly add the buttermilk and process until the dressing is smooth and creamy. Add the vinegar, salt, hot sauce, and black pepper and process for 30 seconds. You should have about 1 1/2 cups of dressing. Place the dressing in a container, cover, and refrigerate.

2. Preheat an oven broiler or set an outdoor grill to high heat. Cover a broiler tray with foil, and coat it with nonstick cooking spray (or coat the grill rack with cooking spray). With a sharp knife, make three diagonal slashes spaced several inches apart on one side of the flank steak. This will prevent the steak from curling while cooking. Place the steak on the broiler pan or directly on the grill about 4 to 5 inches from the heat source. Cook for 11 to 12 minutes for medium, turning once. Cook longer to your liking. Remove the steak from the grill, put it on a plate, and tent it with foil to keep warm.

3. Combine the mixed greens, red pepper, red onion, cherry tomatoes, and basil in a large bowl. Set aside.

4. Add the pumpkin seeds to a small dry skillet. Toast the seeds over medium heat for 3 to 4 minutes, shaking the pan occasionally until lightly browned. Watch carefully so they don't burn. Set aside.

5. Thinly slice the flank steak. Add 2 tablespoons of the dressing to the salad green mixture and toss well. Divide the salad among 6 plates. Top with the sliced steak. Drizzle with an additional 1 tablespoon of dressing per serving. Garnish with pumpkin seeds.

COOK'S TIP | You will have leftover dressing for another use. Store in an airtight container and use within 1 week.

FLANK STEAK SALAD WITH CREAMY HERB DRESSING

Calories 140	Total Fat 6 g	Cholesterol 25 mg	Total Carbohydrate 6 g	Protein 17 g
Calories from Fat 55	Saturated Fat 2 g	Sodium 160 mg	Dietary Fiber 2 g	Phosphorus 175 mg
	Trans Fat 0 g	Potassium 410 mg	Sugars 3 g	

CREAMY HERB DRESSING ONLY

Calories 10	Total Fat 0 g	Cholesterol 0 mg	Total Carbohydrate 1 g	Protein 0 g
Calories from Fat 0	Saturated Fat 0 g	Sodium 90 mg	Dietary Fiber 0g	Phosphorus 10 mg
	Trans Fat 0g	Potassium 20 mg	Sugars 1g	

ITALIAN TOMATO SAUCE

1 1/2 tablespoons olive oil

1 medium onion, chopped

2 garlic cloves, minced

1 medium carrot, peeled and diced

1/2 cup minced fresh flat-leafed parsley

1 (28-ounce) can whole tomatoes with the juice

Kosher salt and fresh-ground black pepper to taste

Pinch of sugar

3 tablespoons minced fresh basil

1 Heat the oil in a large skillet over medium-low heat. Add the onion, garlic, and carrot, and sauté them very gently for 10 to 12 minutes, or until soft.

2 Add the parsley to the sautéed vegetables, and continue to cook for 2 more minutes. Add the tomatoes with the juice to a large bowl. Using your hands, crush the tomatoes coarsely.

3 Add the tomatoes to the skillet, and raise the heat to medium high. Cook until the liquid evaporates, about 20 minutes, and the sauce looks thick. Season with salt, pepper, and a pinch of sugar. Add in the basil, and cook for 1 minute.

4 Serve over cooked pasta.*

Rigatoni pictured is not included in nutritional analysis.

205

Calories 85	Total Fat 4.5 g	Cholesterol 0 mg	Total Carbohydrate 11 g	Protein 2 g
Calories from Fat 40	Saturated Fat 0.6 g	Sodium 240 mg*	Dietary Fiber 3 g	Phosphorus 45 mg
	Trans Fat 0 g	Potassium 405 mg	Sugars 6 g	

*without added salt

PASTA

PESTO

3 tablespoons olive oil

2 tablespoons low-fat, reduced-sodium chicken broth

4–5 garlic cloves, coarsely chopped

1/4 cup grated fresh Parmesan cheese

2 tablespoons toasted pine nuts

3/4 cup torn basil leaves

Sea salt and freshly ground black pepper to taste

1 In a food processor, add the oil, broth, garlic, cheese, and pine nuts. Puree completely. Add in the basil, and puree again. (By waiting until the end of the processing to add the basil, you should get a rich green pesto rather than a dull brown one.) Season well with salt and pepper.

2 Serve over cooked pasta.*

Pappardelle pictured not included in nutritional analysis.

Calories 50	Total Fat 5 g	Cholesterol 0 mg	Total Carbohydrate 1 g	Protein 1 g
Calories from Fat 45	Saturated Fat 0.9 g	Sodium 20 mg*	Dietary Fiber 0 g	Phosphorus 20 mg
	Trans Fat 0 g	Potassium 30 mg	Sugars 0 g	

*without added salt

PASTA

CREAMY CHEESE SAUCE FOR PASTA ✓

1 tablespoon olive oil

4 garlic cloves, minced

1/4 teaspoon crushed red pepper

1/2 cup rehydrated sliced sun-dried tomatoes

1/2 cup pasta water (reserve this after the pasta has been cooked and drained)

2 tablespoons grated fresh Parmesan cheese

1/2 cup low-fat ricotta cheese (such as Figro)

1/3 cup reduced-fat goat cheese

2 tablespoons diced prosciutto

2 tablespoons minced parsley

Kosher salt and fresh-ground black pepper to taste

1 Heat the oil over medium-high heat in a large skillet. Add the garlic, crushed red pepper, sun-dried tomatoes, and pasta water. Cover and cook for 5 minutes.

2 Add the Parmesan, ricotta, goat cheese, and prosciutto to a large bowl. Add in the garlic-tomato mixture. Add the parsley, and season with salt and pepper. Toss with cooked pasta.*

Orecchiette pictured not included in nutritional analysis.

Calories 55	Total Fat 3.5 g	Cholesterol 5 mg	Total Carbohydrate 3 g	Protein 4 g
Calories from Fat 30	Saturated Fat 1.3 g	Sodium 145 mg*	Dietary Fiber 0 g	Phosphorus 65 mg
	Trans Fat 0 g	Potassium 155 mg	Sugars 2 g	

*without added salt

PENNE WITH FRESH TOMATO HERB SAUCE

1 tablespoon olive oil

1 onion, chopped

1 carrot, diced

1 leek, white part only, diced

1 celery stalk, diced

3 garlic cloves, thinly sliced

4 plum tomatoes, seeded and diced

1 (35-ounce) can Roma

...in

...aste

...y

...resh

1 Heat the oil in a large skillet over medium heat. Add the onion, carrot, leek, and celery and sauté for 8 minutes. Add the garlic and sauté for 1 minute. Add the tomatoes and bay leaf. Season with salt and pepper to taste. Cook, uncovered, for 15 to 20 minutes.

2 Meanwhile, bring a large pot of water to a boil. Add the pasta until cooked al dente, about 7 to 8 minutes.

3 Remove the bay leaf from the sauce. Add the parsley, basil, and oregano. Taste and adjust the seasonings. Add the olives.

4 Drain the pasta, add the sauce, and toss gently. Top with Parmesan cheese.

Calories 280	Total Fat 4 g	Cholesterol 5 mg	Total Carbohydrate 55 g	Protein 10 g
35	Saturated Fat 0.9 g	Sodium 250 mg*	Dietary Fiber 9 g	Phosphorus 205 mg
	Trans Fat 0 g	Potassium 550 mg	Sugars 8 g	

*without added salt

PASTA WITH ROASTED ASPARAGUS

ROASTED ASPARAGUS

- 1 pound fresh asparagus, tough ends removed and stalks cut diagonally into 1-inch lengths
- 2 teaspoons olive oil
- 1 teaspoon fresh lemon juice
- Salt and pepper to taste

PASTA

- 8 ounces whole-wheat penne or other shaped pasta (choose a low-carb brand if desired; not included in nutritional analysis)
- 1 teaspoon olive oil
- 1/2 cup diced onion
- 3 garlic cloves, minced
- 1/4 cup coarsely chopped walnuts
- Pinch red pepper flakes (add more if you like your food hotter; not included in nutritional analysis)
- 2 tablespoons minced fresh parsley

GARNISHES

- 1 ounce reduced-fat goat cheese, crumbled
- 2 tablespoons fresh grated Parmesan cheese
- Salt and pepper to taste

1 Prepare the asparagus: Preheat the oven to 450°F. Toss the asparagus with the olive oil, lemon juice, and salt and pepper. Arrange the asparagus in a single layer on a baking sheet and roast in the oven for about 7 to 8 minutes until browned. Remove the asparagus from the oven.

2 For the pasta, cook the pasta according to package directions. Meanwhile, in a large skillet, heat the olive oil. Add the onion and garlic, and sauté for 3 minutes. Add in the walnuts and sauté for 2 minutes. Add in the red pepper flakes and parsley. Drain the pasta, reserving about $1/2$ to $3/4$ cup of the cooking liquid.

3 Add the pasta to the onion-garlic-walnut mixture and toss. Add in the reserved cooking liquid, roasted asparagus, goat cheese, and Parmesan cheese. Add salt and pepper to taste, and toss again.

Calories 200	Total Fat 7 g	Cholesterol 5 mg	Total Carbohydrate 30 g	Protein 7 g
Calories from Fat 65	Saturated Fat 1.3 g	Sodium 45 mg*	Dietary Fiber 5 g	Phosphorus 115 mg
	Trans Fat 0 g	Potassium 150 mg	Sugars 3 g	

*without added salt

IT'S SPRING PASTA SALAD

VINAIGRETTE

- 2 tablespoons red wine vinegar
- 1 garlic clove, finely minced or crushed, almost to a paste
- 1 tablespoon Dijon mustard
- 2 teaspoons fresh lemon juice
- Pinch sugar
- 2 1/2 tablespoons olive oil
- Sea salt and freshly ground black pepper to taste

SALAD

- 1 package (9 ounces) fresh or frozen cheese tortellini
- 2 large carrots, peeled and thinly sliced
- 2 plum tomatoes, diced
- 1 cup frozen green peas, thawed
- 1/3 cup finely chopped red onion

1 Boil the water for the pasta and prepare the vinaigrette. Whisk together the vinegar, garlic, Dijon mustard, lemon juice, and sugar. In a thin stream, slowly add the olive oil, whisking constantly. Season with salt and pepper. Set aside.

2 Cook the tortellini in boiling water for about 6 minutes (or per instructions on the package). Drain well.

3 Add the pasta to a bowl, and add the carrots, tomatoes, peas, and red onion. Pour the dressing over the pasta and vegetables, tossing gently to coat. Cover and refrigerate for 30 minutes before serving.

215

Calories 165	Total Fat 7 g	Cholesterol 10 mg	Total Carbohydrate 20 g	Protein 6 g
Calories from Fat 65	Saturated Fat 1.5 g	Sodium 215 mg*	Dietary Fiber 3 g	Phosphorus 95 mg
	Trans Fat 0 g	Potassium 170 mg	Sugars 3 g	

*without added salt

OVEN-BAKED CAVATAPPI WITH RED PEPPERS AND RICOTTA

1 pound cavatappi, fusilli, or penne pasta

SAUCE

1 teaspoon olive oil

1/4 pound diced prosciutto

3 medium red peppers, seeded, cored, and diced

1 large onion, diced

4 garlic cloves, minced

2 teaspoons dried oregano

1/4 teaspoon crushed red pepper flakes

1 (14.5-ounce) can diced tomatoes, drained

1 tablespoon fresh minced thyme

1 1/2 cups 1% milk

1/4 cup flour

15 ounces part-skim ricotta cheese

1/4 cup Pecorino Romano cheese

Pinch nutmeg

Kosher or sea salt and fresh-ground black pepper to taste

TOPPING

2 slices whole-wheat bread, crusts removed

1/4 cup grated Pecorino Romano cheese

Kosher or sea salt and fresh-ground pepper to taste

1 teaspoon olive oil

1 Cook the pasta according to package directions, but no more than about 6 to 7 minutes. You want the pasta very al dente, as it will continue to bake in the oven. Drain and set aside.

2 Heat the olive oil in a large skillet over medium heat. Add the prosciutto and sauté for 3 minutes. Add in the peppers, onion, and garlic, and sauté for 6 to 7 minutes or until tender. Add in the oregano and crushed red pepper, and sauté for 1 minute. Add in the tomatoes and cook for 2 minutes. Remove the pepper-tomato mixture from the heat, and stir in the thyme. Set aside.

3 Preheat the oven to 450°F. In a large bowl, whisk together the milk and flour until very smooth. Add in the ricotta and the first 1/4 cup of Pecorino Romano cheese, and continue to whisk until very smooth. Add in the nutmeg, salt, and pepper.

4 Combine the cooked pasta with the pepper-tomato mixture and stir well. Add in the ricotta mixture and mix well. Pour the pasta into a 13-inch shallow baking pan (preferably only 2 inches deep). A shallow pan provides more surface area for a crispy crust and allows the interior to cook through more quickly, keeping the sauce moist.

5 Prepare the topping: In a food processor or blender, make crumbs of the whole wheat bread. You should have about a cup. Combine the crumbs with the Pecorino Romano cheese, salt, and pepper, and drizzle with olive oil. Sprinkle the topping on the pasta, and bake uncovered for 25 minutes. Serve immediately.

217

Calories 210	Total Fat 5 g	Cholesterol 15 mg	Total Carbohydrate 30 g	Protein 11 g
Calories from Fat 45	Saturated Fat 2.3 g	Sodium 235 mg*	Dietary Fiber 2 g	Phosphorus 170 mg
	Trans Fat 0 g	Potassium 245 mg	Sugars 5 g	

*without added salt

CHICKEN POT PIE WITH PHYLLO

2 cups low-fat, reduced-sodium chicken broth

1/2 cup water

1 pound small unpeeled red potatoes, cut into quarters

3 sprigs fresh thyme

3 medium carrots, diced into 1/2-inch pieces

1 large onion, diced

1 pound boneless, skinless chicken breasts, diced into 1/2-inch pieces

1 1/2 cups 1% milk

1/2 cup half-and-half

6 tablespoons flour

Kosher salt or sea salt and fresh-ground black pepper to taste

8 ounces frozen peas

8 (14 9-inch) sheets phyllo dough

Butter-flavored spray

1 In a 2-quart saucepan, bring the chicken broth and water to a boil. Add in the potatoes and thyme leaves, and lower the heat to medium. Simmer the potatoes for about 8 minutes or until tender. With a slotted spoon, remove the potatoes and thyme to a bowl. Discard the thyme leaves. Add the carrots and onion to the stock, and simmer for 4 minutes. With a slotted spoon, remove the carrots and onion to the same bowl with the potatoes.

2 Add the chicken to the stock, and simmer for 3 minutes. With a slotted spoon, remove the chicken to the same bowl with the vegetables. Boil the stock until reduced to a cup.

3 Meanwhile, whisk the milk, half-and-half, and flour together in a bowl until very smooth. When the stock is reduced, slowly add the milk mixture, constantly stirring until thickened but still smooth. Add the sauce to the vegetables, and season with salt and pepper. Add in the peas and mix well.

4 Pour the mixture into a 9×13-inch pan. Set aside.

5 Prepare the phyllo dough topping: Spread one sheet of phyllo out onto a very lightly floured surface. Be sure to cover the remaining sheets of phyllo with a towel to avoid exposing to air; the phyllo will crack if exposed. Coat with the butter spray. Add another sheet of phyllo on top of the first and coat with spray. Repeat this process until all 8 sheets are used.

6 Carefully lift the phyllo dough stack and place over the chicken-vegetable filling. Tuck the edges under. With a sharp knife, make 3 diagonal slashes across the top of the dough. This will allow steam to escape.

7 Bake the chicken pot pie, uncovered, at 350°F for about 30 minutes or until the top is puffed and golden brown. Remove from the oven and let stand for about 5 minutes. Cut into squares.

Calories 175	Total Fat 3 g	Cholesterol 25 mg	Total Carbohydrate 25 g	Protein 13 g
Calories from Fat 25	Saturated Fat 1.2 g	Sodium 180 mg*	Dietary Fiber 3 g	Phosphorus 175 mg
	Trans Fat 0 g	Potassium 415 mg	Sugars 5 g	

*without added salt

PROVENÇAL ZUCCHINI AND YELLOW SQUASH MEDLEY

1 tablespoon olive oil

1/2 cup chopped onion

1 large zucchini, cut into 1-inch cubes

1 large yellow squash, cut into 1-inch cubes

2 garlic cloves, minced

1 teaspoon Herbes de Provence,* crushed

1/2 cup halved cherry tomatoes

Salt and pepper to taste

1/4 cup feta cheese

Herbes de Provence is a blend of dried basil, fennel seed, marjoram, rosemary, sage, summer savory, and thyme. It is available in many supermarkets in the spice section. If unavailable, use one or two of these herbs to equal 1 teaspoon.

1 Preheat oven broiler. Heat the oil in a large skillet over medium-high heat. Add the onion and sauté for 3 minutes. Add the zucchini and yellow squash, and sauté for 5 to 6 minutes. Add the garlic and sauté for 2 more minutes.

2 Add the Herbes de Provence, cherry tomatoes, and salt and pepper. Transfer the vegetable mixture to a small casserole dish. Sprinkle with feta cheese.

3 Place the casserole dish under the broiler for a few minutes until the feta cheese melts.

221

Calories 55	Total Fat 3.5 g	Cholesterol 5 mg	Total Carbohydrate 5 g	Protein 2 g
Calories from Fat 30	Saturated Fat 1.1 g	Sodium 65 mg*	Dietary Fiber 1 g	Phosphorus 60 mg
	Trans Fat 0.1 g	Potassium 295 mg	Sugars 3 g	
				*without added salt

CHEESY BROCCOLI AND RICE CASSEROLE

2 1/2 teaspoons olive oil, divided

1 1/4 cups quick-cooking brown rice

4 cups low-fat, reduced-sodium chicken broth

1 (12-ounce) can low-fat evaporated milk

3 pounds fresh broccoli, cut into bite-sized florets, stems discarded

1 large onion, minced

2 garlic cloves, minced

2/3 cup shredded 50% light cheddar cheese (such as Cabot)

Pinch cayenne pepper

1/4 teaspoon dry mustard

Kosher salt and fresh-ground black pepper to taste

3 tablespoons freshly grated Parmesan or Romano cheese

1 Coat a 9×13-inch casserole dish with cooking spray and set aside. Bring a large pot of lightly salted water to a boil. Meanwhile, heat 1 teaspoon of the olive oil in a large Dutch oven over medium heat. Add the dry rice and sauté for 1 to 2 minutes. Add in the broth and the evaporated milk, and bring to a boil. Cover and simmer on low heat for about 20 minutes, until the rice is tender.

2 Add the broccoli to the pot of boiling water, turn off the heat, and let the broccoli stand in the water for 2 minutes. Drain.

3 Preheat the oven to 400°F. Heat the remaining olive oil in a large skillet. Add the onion, and sauté for 3 minutes. Add in the garlic and broccoli, and sauté for 2 minutes.

4 When the rice is cooked, add in the broccoli-onion mixture, cheddar cheese, cayenne pepper, dry mustard, salt, and pepper. Pour the mixture into the prepared casserole dish. Sprinkle with Parmesan or Romano cheese. Bake for 15 minutes, or until the casserole is bubbly.

Calories 250
Calories from Fat 55

Total Fat 6 g
Saturated Fat 2.3 g
Trans Fat 0 g

Cholesterol 10 mg
Sodium 430 mg*
Potassium 680 mg

Total Carbohydrate 38 g
Dietary Fiber 4 g
Sugars 9 g

Protein 14 g
Phosphorus 345 mg

*without added salt

BISCUIT AND HAMBURGER PIE

FILLING

1/2 pound (93%) lean ground beef

2 teaspoons olive oil

1 large onion, chopped

2 celery stalks, diced

1 medium red bell pepper, seeded, cored, and diced

1 tablespoon all-purpose flour

1 can (14-ounce) low-fat, reduced-sodium beef broth

1/2 cup prepared barbecue sauce

1/2 teaspoon Worcestershire sauce

Kosher salt and fresh-ground black pepper to taste

BISCUIT CRUST

1/2 cup all-purpose flour

1/2 cup whole-wheat pastry flour

1 teaspoon baking powder

1/2 teaspoon baking soda

1/4 teaspoon salt

2 tablespoons minced fresh parsley

1/2 cup low-fat buttermilk

2 tablespoons olive oil

1 Add the ground beef to a large skillet over medium-high heat, and cook until browned, about 3 to 4 minutes. Add to a colander to drain off excess juices.

2 Meanwhile, add the olive oil to the skillet. Sauté the onion, celery, and red pepper for about 8 to 9 minutes, until soft and lightly browned. Add the flour, and sauté for 1 minute. Add the broth, barbecue sauce, Worcestershire sauce, and beef. Cook over medium heat for 10 minutes, or until thickened. Season with salt and pepper. Add the mixture to a 9-inch deep-dish pie pan. Set aside.

3 Preheat the oven to 450°F.

4 To make the crust: In a medium bowl, combine the flours, baking powder, baking soda, salt, and parsley. In a small cup, mix together the buttermilk and olive oil. Make a well in the center of the flour mixture, and pour in the buttermilk-oil mixture. Stir with a fork. Turn the dough out onto a floured surface, and knead about 7 to 8 times. Using a floured rolling pin, roll the dough out into a large circle. Cut the dough into 8 triangles.

5 Lay the biscuit dough on top of the hamburger mixture. Bake the casserole for about 20 to 25 minutes until the biscuits are brown and the casserole is bubbly.

225

Calories 190	Total Fat 7 g	Cholesterol 20 mg	Total Carbohydrate 24 g	Protein 9 g
Calories from Fat 65	Saturated Fat 1.6 g	Sodium 510 mg*	Dietary Fiber 2 g	Phosphorus 180 mg
	Trans Fat 0.1 g	Potassium 330 mg	Sugars 7 g	

*without added salt

CREAMY TUNA NOODLE CASSEROLE

2 slices whole-wheat bread

3 teaspoons olive oil, divided

1 tablespoon grated fresh Parmesan cheese

6 ounces dried wide egg noodles

1 large onion, chopped

2 celery stalks, diced

1 medium red bell pepper, cored, seeded, and diced

2 garlic cloves, minced

2 tablespoons all-purpose flour

2 cups 1% milk

1/2 teaspoon mustard powder

1/2 cup nonfat mayonnaise

7 ounces white tuna in water, drained

1/2 cup grated 50% light extra sharp cheddar cheese (such as Cabot)

2 tablespoons minced fresh basil

Kosher salt and fresh-ground

Black pepper to taste

1 Preheat the oven to 350°F. Remove the crusts from the slices of whole wheat bread. Add the bread to a food processor or blender, and pulse until medium crumbs form. Add the crumbs to a bowl, and add 1 teaspoon of the olive oil and the Parmesan cheese; set aside. Coat a 3-quart casserole dish with cooking spray; set aside.

2 Cook the noodles in boiling water until al dente, about 6 minutes. Drain and set aside. Meanwhile, heat the remaining olive oil in a large skillet over medium heat. Sauté the onion, celery, red pepper, and garlic for about 5 minutes. Add in the flour, and cook for about 1 minute. Add in the milk, and bring to a boil. Cook for about 4 to 5 minutes until thickened. Remove from the heat. Stir in the mustard powder, mayonnaise, tuna, cheese, and basil. Season with salt and pepper.

3 Add in the noodles and mix well. Add the tuna-noodle mixture into the prepared pan. Sprinkle the bread crumb mixture over the casserole. Bake for about 20 to 30 minutes until topping is browned and casserole is bubbling.

227

Calories 230	Total Fat 6 g	Cholesterol 35 mg	Total Carbohydrate 30 g	Protein 14 g
Calories from Fat 55	Saturated Fat 2.1 g	Sodium 300 mg*	Dietary Fiber 3 g	Phosphorus 220 mg
	Trans Fat 0 g	Potassium 315 mg	Sugars 7 g	

*without added salt

PIZZA

GREEK-STYLE PIZZA

10 ounces refrigerated pizza dough

1 tablespoon olive oil, divided

3 garlic cloves, finely minced

2 teaspoons minced fresh oregano

1/2 cup bottled low-fat pizza sauce

1/2 cup reduced-fat crumbled feta cheese

2 tablespoons toasted pine nuts

2 tablespoons chopped pitted Kalamata olives (or any other black olives)

1 Preheat the oven to 425°F. Unroll the dough onto a round pizza pan that has been coated with cooking spray. Brush with half the oil. Bake for 10 minutes. Remove from the oven.

2 Meanwhile, heat the remaining oil. Add the garlic and sauté for 1 minute. Add the oregano and sauté for 1 more minute. Spread the garlic-oregano mixture onto the pizza crust.

3 Spread the pizza sauce evenly onto the crust, leaving a 1/4-inch border. Sprinkle the feta cheese over the sauce and top with pine nuts and olives. Bake the pizza for 8 to 10 minutes until the cheese slightly melts and the crust is golden.

229

Calories 145	**Total Fat 6 g**	**Cholesterol 0 mg**	**Total Carbohydrate 19 g**	**Protein 5 g**
Calories from Fat 55	Saturated Fat 1.4 g	**Sodium 450 mg**	Dietary Fiber 1 g	**Phosphorus 195 mg**
	Trans Fat 0 g	**Potassium 140 mg**	Sugars 3 g	

PIZZA

EASY PIZZA MARGHERITA

10 ounces refrigerated pizza dough

2 teaspoons olive oil

2 garlic cloves, peeled; 1 left whole, 1 sliced thin

6 plum tomatoes, thinly sliced

2/3 cup shredded part-skim mozzarella cheese

1/2 cup basil leaves

1 Preheat the oven to 425°F. Unroll the dough onto a baking sheet that has been coated with cooking spray. Form the dough into a 13×11-inch rectangle. Brush with the olive oil. Bake the crust for 10 minutes. Rub the crust with the whole garlic clove.

2 Arrange the remaining sliced garlic clove on the crust. Top with tomato slices and sprinkle with cheese. Bake for about 8 minutes. Arrange the basil leaves over the pizza and return to the oven for about 2 more minutes until cheese melts and the crust is golden.

231

Calories 130	**Total Fat 4 g**	**Cholesterol 5 mg**	**Total Carbohydrate 19 g**	**Protein 6 g**
Calories from Fat 35	Saturated Fat 1.4 g	**Sodium 315 mg**	Dietary Fiber 1 g	**Phosphorus 200 mg**
	Trans Fat 0 g	**Potassium 190 mg**	Sugars 4 g	

ARTICHOKE AND LEEK PIZZA

10 ounces refrigerated pizza dough

1 tablespoon olive oil, divided

1 large onion, thinly sliced (about 2 cups)

1 large leek, white part only, rinsed well and thinly sliced (about 1 cup)

1 (13.5-ounce) can small artichoke hearts, halved

1/2 teaspoon dried oregano

Pinch red pepper flakes

Salt and pepper to taste

1/4 cup plus 1 tablespoon freshly grated Parmesan cheese, divided

1 Preheat the oven to 425°F. Unroll the dough onto a round pizza pan that has been coated with cooking spray. Form the dough into a pizza crust, building up the edges. Brush the crust with half the oil and bake for 10 minutes. Remove from the oven.

2 Meanwhile, heat the remaining oil. Add the onions and leeks and sauté on medium-low heat for about 20 minutes until golden brown. Add the artichoke hearts, oregano, red pepper flakes, salt, and pepper. Sauté for 2 minutes.

3 Spread the pizza with half of the Parmesan cheese. Top with the artichoke-leek mixture. Sprinkle with the remaining Parmesan cheese. Bake for about 8 to 10 minutes until crust is browned and cheese is melted.

Calories 145	**Total Fat 4 g**	**Cholesterol 5 mg**	**Total Carbohydrate 24 g**	**Protein 5 g**
Calories from Fat 35	Saturated Fat 1.1 g	**Sodium 370 mg***	Dietary Fiber 1 g	**Phosphorus 195 mg**
	Trans Fat 0 g	**Potassium 195 mg**	Sugars 4 g	

*without added salt

PIZZA

MEXICAN PIZZA

2 (6-inch) corn tortillas

1/3 cup canned fat-free refried beans

2 tablespoons sliced mini sweet and/or jalapeño peppers

1/4 cup hot or mild salsa

1 tablespoon 50% reduced-fat shredded sharp cheddar cheese, such as Cabot

1/4 teaspoon olive oil

This is a high-sodium dish. Look for salsa and beans with the least sodium per serving.

1 Preheat the oven or toaster oven to 375°F. Place the tortillas on a baking sheet or toaster oven tray. Spread the tortillas with refried beans, lay on the pepper slices, top with salsa, sprinkle with cheese, and drizzle with olive oil.

2 Bake for 10 minutes, or until the cheese is melted and the tortillas are crisp.

Calories 220	**Total Fat 4 g**	**Cholesterol 5 mg**	**Total Carbohydrate 38 g**	**Protein 10 g**
Calories from Fat 35	Saturated Fat 1 g	**Sodium 805 mg**	Dietary Fiber 8 g	**Phosphorus 305 mg**
	Trans Fat 0 g	**Potassium 600 mg**	Sugars 4 g	

DESSERTS

PEAR-WALNUT CRUMBLE

4 large pears, unpeeled and cut into 1/2-inch-wide slices

1/4 cup Splenda for baking

2 tablespoons orange juice

2 teaspoons orange zest

CRUMBLE

1/2 cup whole-wheat pastry flour

1/2 cup old-fashioned rolled oats (not instant)

1/3 cup brown sugar substitute (Splenda)

1 tablespoon butter

1 tablespoon canola oil

2 tablespoons orange juice concentrate

2 tablespoons chopped walnuts

1 Preheat the oven to 375°F.

2 Coat a 2-quart baking dish with cooking spray. In a bowl, toss the pears, Splenda, orange juice, and orange zest and add to the baking dish.

3 In another bowl, combine the flour, oats, and brown sugar. Add the butter and work the butter in with your fingertips or a pastry blender until the mixture resembles coarse crumbs. Add the oil and mix well. Add in the orange juice concentrate until the mixture is moistened.

4 Spread the crumble mixture evenly over the pears. Bake for about 25 minutes. Top the crumble with the walnuts and continue to bake for another 20 minutes until pears are soft and topping is browned.

Calories 190	Total Fat 4.5 g	Cholesterol 5 mg	Total Carbohydrate 37 g	Protein 2 g
Calories from Fat 40	Saturated Fat 1.1 g	Sodium 10 mg	Dietary Fiber 4 g	Phosphorus 60 mg
	Trans Fat 0.1 g	Potassium 215 mg	Sugars 23 g	

APPLE CAKE WITH LEMON THYME

1 tart large apple (e.g., Granny Smith), about 1 1/2 cups, cubed and peeled

4 tablespoons finely chopped, fresh thyme leaves (try to use lemon thyme if you can find it)

1 tablespoon fresh lemon juice

2 cups unbleached all-purpose flour

3/4 cup Splenda

1 1/2 teaspoons baking powder

3/4 teaspoon baking soda

3/4 teaspoon cinnamon

1/2 teaspoon nutmeg

1/8 teaspoon salt

2 eggs, lightly beaten

1/3 cup canola oil

1/4 cup orange juice

1 teaspoon vanilla

1 Preheat the oven to 350°F. Lightly coat with nonstick spray and flour an 8×8-inch square pan. Combine the apples, thyme, and lemon juice, and set aside.

2 Combine the flour, Splenda, baking powder, baking soda, cinnamon, nutmeg, and salt in a separate bowl. In a large bowl combine the eggs, oil, orange juice, and vanilla.

3 Add the apple-thyme mixture to the egg mixture, and mix until blended. Add dry ingredients, stirring until just combined. Spoon batter into prepared pan and bake for 30 minutes. Allow to cool, and serve.

239

Calories 240	Total Fat 11 g	Cholesterol 55 mg	Total Carbohydrate 31 g	Protein 5 g
Calories from Fat 100	Trans Fat 0 g	Sodium 240 mg	Dietary Fiber 2 g	Phosphorus 150 mg
	Saturated Fat 1.1 g	Potassium 100 mg	Sugars 7 g	

APPLE LEMON RAISIN STRUDEL

1 1/2 tablespoons light butter, melted

1/2 cup Splenda brown sugar, divided

2 tablespoons dry plain bread crumbs

3/4 teaspoon cinnamon

4 cups thinly sliced and peeled apples (any except Red Delicious)

1/4 cup raisins or currants

1/2 teaspoon grated lemon zest

8 sheets (9 14-inch) frozen phyllo pastry, thawed (thaw at room temperature for 2 hours)

Cooking spray

1/2 teaspoon sugar

1 Preheat the oven to 350°F.

2 Pour the butter into a small bowl or custard cup.

3 Combine the bread crumbs, cinnamon, and half of the brown sugar in a small bowl

4 Toss the apples, ¼ cup brown sugar, raisins or currants, and lemon zest in a large bowl.

5 Place 2 phyllo sheets on a large cutting board or work surface (cover the remaining dough to keep from drying out), covered with parchment paper for easier cleanup, and lightly brush with the melted butter. Sprinkle with 2 tablespoons of the bread crumb mixture. Repeat the layers with the remaining phyllo, melted butter mixture, and bread crumbs, ending with phyllo. Lightly coat the top phyllo sheet with cooking spray. Arrange the apple mixture over the phyllo, leaving a 2-inch border. Be careful not to use any of the liquid at the bottom of the bowl or the strudel will become soggy. Starting at the short edge, roll up the phyllo jelly-roll style. Do not roll too tightly or the phyllo will split. Place the strudel, seam-side down, on a baking sheet coated with cooking spray or covered with parchment paper. Lightly spray strudel with cooking spray, and sprinkle with remaining brown sugar.

6 Bake for 30 minutes or until golden. Cool for 10 minutes and remove from the pan. Cut with a serrated knife.

241

Calories 120	Total Fat 1 g	Cholesterol 0 mg	Total Carbohydrate 26 g	Protein 1 g
Calories from Fat 10	Saturated Fat 0.2 g	Sodium 60 mg	Dietary Fiber 1 g	Phosphorus 20 mg
	Trans Fat 0 g	Potassium 90 mg	Sugars 18 g	

DESSERTS

SUPER BANANA SUNDAES

1 1/3 cups fat-free vanilla ice cream (such as Breyers Double Churned Free)

1/3 cup crushed graham crackers

1 medium banana, peeled and sliced

1/4 cup fat-free whipped topping

GARNISH

4 strawberries, sliced

1 Place 1/3 cup of the ice cream into a dessert dish. Layer 1/4 of the remaining ingredients on top of the ice cream. Repeat with other sundaes.

2 Top with sliced strawberries and serve immediately.

Calories 130	Total Fat 1 g	Cholesterol 0 mg	Total Carbohydrate 29 g	Protein 3 g
Calories from Fat 10	Saturated Fat 0.1 g	Sodium 80 mg	Dietary Fiber 3 g	Phosphorus 85 mg
	Trans Fat 0 g	Potassium 280 mg	Sugars 15 g	

DESSERTS

RASPBERRY ICE CREAM FLOATS

2 cups fresh raspberries

1/2 teaspoon Splenda sugar substitute

2 1/2 cups no-sugar-added, reduced-fat vanilla ice cream (such as Breyers Double Churned No Sugar Added French Vanilla)

3 1/2 cups low-sodium club soda

1 Press the raspberries through a fine sieve over a small bowl and discard the seeds. Combine the raspberry pulp and Splenda.

2 Divide the raspberry mixture evenly among four 8-ounce glasses.

3 Spoon 2 tablespoons of the ice cream into each glass. Stir in 2 tablespoons of the club soda. Top with about 1/2 cup more of the ice cream and pour in about 3/4 cup of club soda over the ice cream. Serve immediately.

Calories 140	Total Fat 6 g	Cholesterol 40 mg	Total Carbohydrate 24 g	Protein 3 g
Calories from Fat 55	Saturated Fat 3.1 g	Sodium 125 mg	Dietary Fiber 9 g	Phosphorus 95 mg
	Trans Fat 0 g	Potassium 255 mg	Sugars 8 g	

DESSERTS

FROZEN DOUBLE FUDGE PEANUT BUTTER PIE

CRUST

15 graham crackers

2 1/2 tablespoons light butter (such as Land O' Lakes Light Butter, 50% less fat)

FILLING

4 1/2 cups fat-free chocolate ice cream (such as Breyers Double Churned Fat-Free French Chocolate)

3 tablespoons reduced-fat smooth peanut butter

3 tablespoons fat-free chocolate syrup

1 tablespoon fat-free milk

1 1/2 cups fat-free whipped topping (such as Cool Whip Free)

1 Preheat the oven to 350°F. In a food processor, process the graham crackers until fine crumbs form. Add the crumbs to a bowl, and add the melted butter. Combine well. Press the crumb mixture into a nonstick 9-inch pie pan to form a crust. Bake for 7 minutes. Remove the crust from the oven and place on a rack to cool for 15 minutes. Freeze the crust for 15 minutes.

2 As the pie crust is chilling, remove the ice cream from the freezer to soften for about 10 to 15 minutes. Combine the peanut butter, chocolate syrup, and milk; mix until smooth. Remove the crust from the freezer. Add 2 cups of ice cream into the crust. Spread with the peanut butter mixture. Top with remaining ice cream. Cover and freeze for 3 hours.

3 Remove the pie from the freezer and allow to soften for 5 minutes. Spoon whipped topping over pie and serve.

Calories 205	Total Fat 4.5 g	Cholesterol 5 mg	Total Carbohydrate 38 g	Protein 5 g
Calories from Fat 40	Saturated Fat 1.4 g	Sodium 175 mg	Dietary Fiber 4 g	Phosphorus 125 mg
	Trans Fat 0 g	Potassium 230 mg	Sugars 20 g	

SIMPLE AND ELEGANT POACHED PEARS

1 cup red wine or low-calorie cranberry juice

1 cup water

2 tablespoons sugar

1/2 teaspoon vanilla

1 slice lemon

6 small, ripe, but firm pears, peeled, stems intact (D'Anjou are best)

1 In a large Dutch oven or large saucepan, combine the wine or juice, water, sugar, vanilla, and lemon slice. Bring to a simmer.

2 Add the pears and submerge them as much as possible. Bring the mixture to a boil, lower the heat, and cook over low heat about 30 to 40 minutes, until the pears are soft when pierced with a cake tester or wooden skewer. Turn the pears occasionally throughout the process for even cooking.

3 Remove the pears from the pan and set aside to cool.

4 Bring the liquid that remains in the pan to a boil and reduce until syrupy.

5 The pears can be served warm with heated poaching liquid poured on top or with both fruit and liquid chilled.

249

Calories 95	Total Fat 0 g	Cholesterol 0 mg	Total Carbohydrate 23 g	Protein 0 g
Calories from Fat 0	Saturated Fat 0 g	Sodium 0 mg	Dietary Fiber 4 g	Phosphorus 15 mg
	Trans Fat 0 g	Potassium 155 mg	Sugars 16 g	

DESSERTS

STRAWBERRY GRANITA

1 pound ripe strawberries, hulled and sliced

2 tablespoons Splenda for baking

1 cup diet cranberry juice drink

Sliced strawberries or raspberries for garnish

1 In a bowl, combine the strawberries and Splenda. Let soak for about 1 hour at room temperature.

2 Add the berries and all accumulated juices to a food processor or blender.

3 Add the cranberry juice to the mixture, place in a shallow metal tray, and freeze for 30 minutes. Using a fork, scrape the frozen edges into the liquid center. Return the tray to the freezer, and freeze for another 30 minutes. Repeat this process about 3 more times until you have a mixture that is fluffy, soft ice crystals.

4 Serve the granita in dessert cups with berries to garnish.

Calories 30	Total Fat 0 g	Cholesterol 0 mg	Total Carbohydrate 7 g	Protein 0 g
Calories from Fat 0	Saturated Fat 0 g	Sodium 5 mg	Dietary Fiber 1 g	Phosphorus 15 mg
	Trans Fat 0 g	Potassium 90 mg	Sugars 6 g	

SERVING SIZE about 1 2 1/2-inch square | SERVES 8
PREP/COOK TIME 10 minutes/20 minutes + 10 minutes to cool
EXCHANGES 1 1/2 Carbohydrate, 1/2 Fat

DOUBLE CHOCOLATE CAKE

1 1/2 cups all-purpose flour

1/2 cup unsweetened cocoa powder

1 teaspoon baking soda

Pinch salt

1/4 cup canola oil

1/4 cup unsweetened applesauce

2 whole eggs

1/2 cup Splenda Sugar Blend

1/4 cup light brown sugar

1 cup low-fat buttermilk

2 teaspoons vanilla

1/3 cup mini chocolate chips

1/4 cup sugar-free chocolate syrup

1 Preheat the oven to 350°F. Coat a 9×13-inch pan with cooking spray. Dust very lightly with a bit of flour.

2 Combine the flour, cocoa powder, baking soda, and pinch of salt in a large bowl. Set aside.

3 In another bowl, beat together the oil and applesauce on medium with an electric mixer. Add the eggs, one at a time, and beat well. Add in half the Splenda and brown sugar alternately with half of the buttermilk to the flour mixture. Repeat until all the buttermilk is used. Add in the vanilla and beat for 30 seconds. Fold in the chocolate chips by hand.

4 Pour the batter into the prepared pan, and bake for about 20 minutes, or until a toothpick inserted in the center comes out clean.

5 Let the cake cool in the pan for about 10 minutes. Cut into squares and place on individual plates. Drizzle with some chocolate syrup, and serve the cake warm or at room temperature.

Calories 135	Total Fat 4.5 g	Cholesterol 20 mg	Total Carbohydrate 21 g	Protein 3 g
Calories from Fat 40	Saturated Fat 1.1 g	Sodium 85 mg*	Dietary Fiber 1 g	Phosphorus 50 mg
	Trans Fat 0 g	Potassium 90 mg	Sugars 12 g	

*without added salt

ESPRESSO ZABAGLIONE

4 egg yolks

1/4 cup sugar

Pinch nutmeg*

2 tablespoons strong espresso coffee or 1 1/2 teaspoons instant espresso powder dissolved in 2 tablespoons warm water

1 tablespoon coffee liqueur (optional)

2 teaspoons grated semisweet chocolate

Not included in nutritional analysis.

1 In a double boiler over simmering water, whisk the egg yolks and sugar until smooth and creamy. Make sure to fill the water so that the bottom of the top pan does not touch the water.

2 Beating constantly with a wire whisk, beat the mixture until it begins to thicken, about 5 minutes. Don't beat the mixture much longer than 5 minutes to avoid overcooking the eggs.

3 Remove the top of the double boiler, and add the nutmeg, espresso, and liqueur if using. Return the pan to the double boiler, and continue to whisk for 3 to 5 more minutes. Remove from the heat, and spoon the zabaglione into dessert dishes. Sprinkle with grated chocolate and serve immediately.

255

Calories 75	**Total Fat 3.5 g**	**Cholesterol 140 mg**	**Total Carbohydrate 9 g**	**Protein 2 g**
Calories from Fat 30	Saturated Fat 1.5 g	**Sodium 0 mg**	Dietary Fiber 0 g	**Phosphorus 45 mg**
	Trans Fat 0 g	**Potassium 20 mg**	Sugars 9 g	

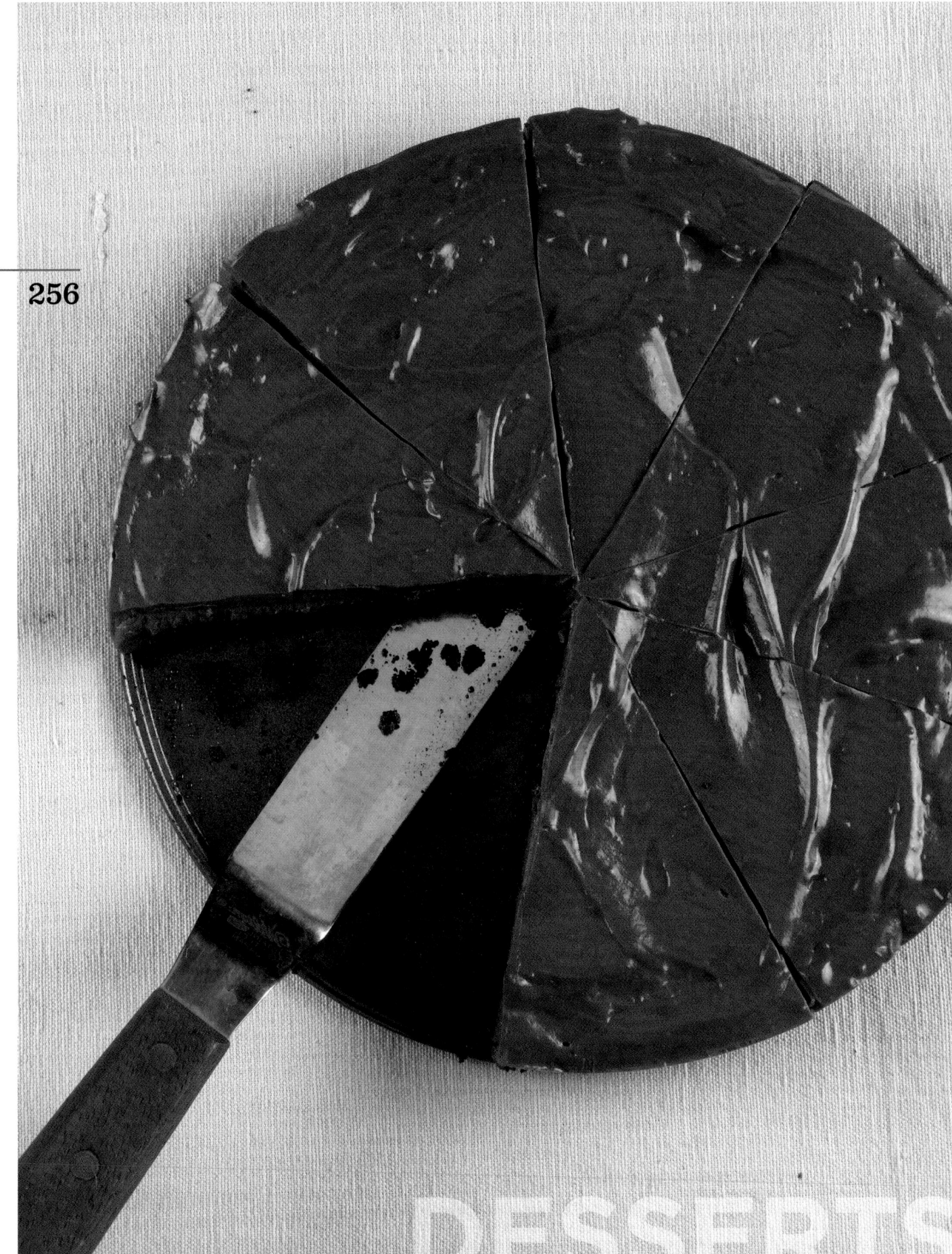

CHOCOLATE CREAM PUDDING PIE

CRUST

1/2 cup sugar-free chocolate wafer cookie crumbs

1 tablespoon sugar

1 tablespoon canola oil

FILLING

3/4 cup Splenda Sugar Blend

1/2 cup cornstarch

1/4 cup cocoa

1/4 teaspoon salt

3 cups fat-free milk

1 egg, lightly beaten

1 teaspoon butter

GARNISH

1/2 cup fat-free whipped topping

1 Preheat the oven to 350°F. Prepare the crust: Mix together the cookie crumbs, sugar, and oil. Pour the mixture into the bottom of an 8-inch springform pan or loose-bottom tart pan. Bake for 10 minutes. Remove from the oven, and cool on a wire rack.

2 Prepare the filling: In a medium saucepan over medium heat, whisk together the Splenda, cornstarch, cocoa, and salt. Slowly whisk in the milk and then the egg. Whisk constantly until the mixture comes to a boil and thickens.

3 Cook and stir 3 minutes more. Remove from the heat. Whisk in the butter. Pour the mixture into a bowl and cover with plastic wrap directly on the surface to prevent the mixture from forming a skin. Let cool for 20 minutes.

4 Remove the plastic wrap, and pour the filling on top of the prepared crust. Refrigerate for 2 hours before serving. Serve with a dollop of whipped topping.

Calories 195	Total Fat 4.5 g	Cholesterol 25 mg	Total Carbohydrate 35 g	Protein 4 g
Calories from Fat 40	Saturated Fat 1.1 g	Sodium 130 mg	Dietary Fiber 1 g	Phosphorus 125 mg
	Trans Fat 0 g	Potassium 185 mg	Sugars 23 g	

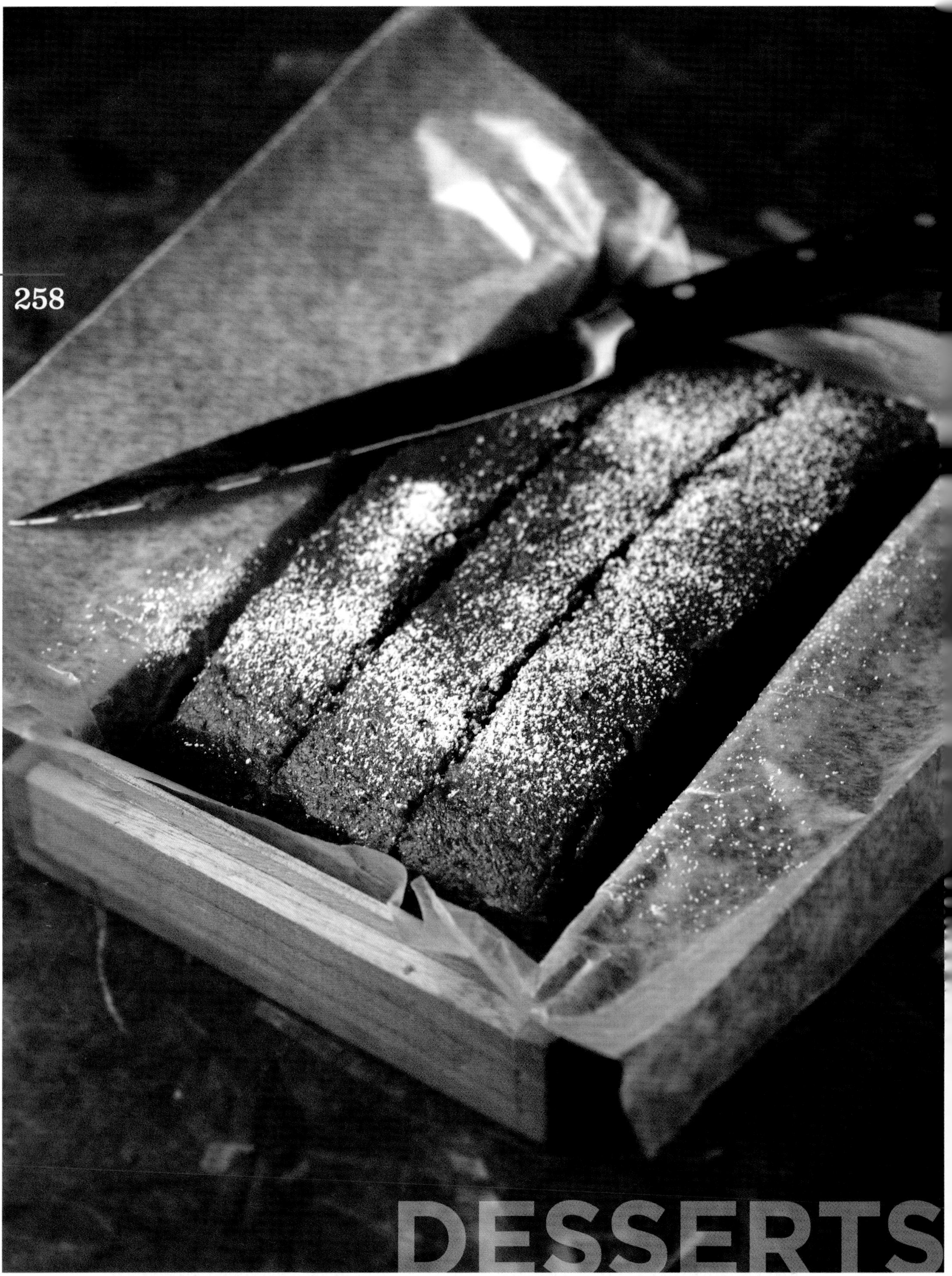

DESSERTS

TRIPLE GINGERBREAD SQUARES

1 cup all-purpose flour

1/4 cup whole-wheat pastry flour

1/2 teaspoon ground ginger

1/2 teaspoon baking soda

1/4 teaspoon salt

1/2 cup Splenda Sugar Blend

1/2 cup low-fat buttermilk

1/4 cup unsweetened applesauce

14 cup molasses

1/4 cup canola oil

1 egg, beaten

2 tablespoons finely minced crystallized ginger

1 teaspoon finely grated fresh ginger

1 1/2 tablespoons powdered sugar

1 Preheat the oven to 350°F. Coat a 9-inch square baking pan with cooking spray. In a large bowl, combine the flours, ground ginger, baking soda, and salt.

2 In another bowl, combine the Splenda with the buttermilk, applesauce, molasses, oil, egg, crystallized ginger, and fresh ginger.

3 Slowly stir in the flour mixture, and mix to combine.

4 Pour the batter into the prepared pan, and bake for 25 minutes, until a toothpick inserted into the gingerbread comes out clean. Cool in the pan. Sprinkle with powdered sugar, and cut into 25 squares.

259

Calories 80	Total Fat 2.5 g	Cholesterol 10 mg	Total Carbohydrate 13 g	Protein 1 g
Calories from Fat 20	Saturated Fat 0.3 g	Sodium 60 mg	Dietary Fiber 0 g	Phosphorus 20 mg
	Trans Fat 0 g	Potassium 70 mg	Sugars 7 g	

DESSERTS

MINT CHOCOLATE CHIP MERINGUES

3 egg whites
1/4 teaspoon cream of tartar
   Pinch of salt
3/4 cup sugar
3 tablespoons unsweetened or Dutch process cocoa
1/3 cup mini chocolate chips
3/4 teaspoon peppermint extract
5 very finely crushed sugar-free peppermint candies

1 Preheat the oven to 250°F.

2 Cover a baking sheet with parchment paper.

3 Beat the egg whites, cream of tartar, and salt with an electric mixer on high until foamy.

4 Combine the sugar and cocoa. Gradually add the cocoa mixture to the egg whites, and beat until stiff peaks form. Gently fold in the chocolate chips, peppermint extract, and crushed candies.

5 Spoon the mixture into a pastry bag fitted with a 1/2-inch round tip.

6 Pipe 30 cookies, 1/4 inch apart, on the prepared baking sheet.

7 Bake the cookies for 1 1/2 hours. Turn the oven off, and let the cookies cool in the oven for 1 hour. Store in a tightly sealed container.

261

Calories 70	Total Fat 1.5 g	Cholesterol 0 mg	Total Carbohydrate 15 g	Protein 1 g
Calories from Fat 15	Saturated Fat 1 g	Sodium 10 mg*	Dietary Fiber 1 g	Phosphorus 15 mg
	Trans Fat 0 g	Potassium 55 mg	Sugars 12 g	

*without added salt

DESSERTS

FUDGE COOKIES

1 cup all-purpose flour

1/2 cup plus 1 tablespoon unsweetened cocoa

1 teaspoon baking powder

1/4 teaspoon salt

1/2 cup butter-flavored spread (such as Smart Balance)

2/3 cup sugar

1/4 cup packed brown sugar

1/3 cup plain low-fat yogurt

1 1/2 teaspoons vanilla extract

1 Preheat the oven to 350°F. Coat two baking sheets with cooking spray.

2 In a medium bowl, combine the flour, cocoa, baking powder, and salt.

3 In a medium saucepan, melt the butter-flavored spread. Add in the sugars; the mixture will be thick. Add in the yogurt and vanilla.

4 In a clean bowl, slowly add the flour mixture to the sugar mixture, stirring to combine. Using level tablespoons, spoon the combined mixture 2 inches apart onto the prepared baking sheets.

5 Bake for about 8 to 10 minutes until almost done. Cool on the sheets until the cookie becomes firm, about 2 to 3 minutes. Transfer to a wire rack to cool completely.

Calories 85	Total Fat 3.5 g	Cholesterol 0 mg	Total Carbohydrate 13 g	Protein 1 g
Calories from Fat 30	Saturated Fat 1 g	Sodium 75 mg	Dietary Fiber 1 g	Phosphorus 45 mg
	Trans Fat 0 g	Potassium 50 mg	Sugars 8 g	

DESSERTS

SERVING SIZE 1/2 cup ice cream, 1 tablespoon sauce, 5 raspberries, 1 tablespoon whipped topping
SERVES 2 | **PREP/COOK TIME** 15 minutes/2 minutes
EXCHANGES 2 Carbohydrate

CHOCOLATE RASPBERRY SUNDAES

CHOCOLATE SAUCE

1/4 cup sugar

3 tablespoons Dutch process cocoa

1/4 cup water

SUNDAES

1 cup fat-free chocolate ice cream, such as Breyers Double Churned French Chocolate

10 fresh raspberries

2 tablespoons fat-free whipped topping*

Not shown in photograph.

1 To make the chocolate sauce, combine the sugar and cocoa in a small saucepan. Whisk well. Slowly add in the water, and combine until smooth. Bring to a boil, lower the heat, and simmer for 2 minutes.

2 For each serving, place 1/2 cup of ice cream in a dessert dish. Drizzle with 1 tablespoon of the sauce.* Top with 5 raspberries and 1 tablespoon of the whipped topping.

There will be some leftover sauce.

Calories 145	Total Fat 0.2 g	Cholesterol 0 mg	Total Carbohydrate 36 g	Protein 4 g
Calories from Fat 0	Saturated Fat 0.2 g	Sodium 60 mg	Dietary Fiber 6 g	Phosphorus 120 mg
	Trans Fat 0 g	Potassium 275 mg	Sugars 23 g	

DESSERTS

DOUBLE-STRAWBERRY MERINGUES

MERINGUES

   2 egg whites

   1/2 cup powdered sugar

   1/4 cup fresh chopped
      strawberries

FRUIT TOPPING

   1 1/2 cups halved
      strawberries

   Mint sprigs

1 Preheat the oven to 250°F. Line a large 13×18-inch cookie sheet with parchment paper. Put the cookie sheet on top of another (this will prevent the meringues from browning too much on the bottom). Set aside.

2 Whip the egg whites with an electric mixer at low speed, about 2 minutes or until they look foamy. Increase the speed to high, and continue beating about 1 1/2 minutes, or until soft peaks form. Gradually beat in the sugar. The whites will become very creamy and glossy, with stiff peaks forming in about 5 to 6 minutes. Gently fold in the strawberries.

3 Using an ice cream scoop, put 1 scoop of the mixture per meringue on the cookie sheet. Each scoop should be about 2 inches in diameter and spaced 1 inch apart from its neighbors. Make a small impression in the center of each meringue.

4 Bake for 1 hour, until the meringue is firm on the outside and light in color. The inside will still be a little moist. Remove from the oven, and let cool for 10 minutes.

5 Loosen the meringues with a spatula, and transfer them to serving plates. Top meringues with the halved strawberries. Garnish with a mint sprig.

COOK'S TIP | If serving only four people, you will have leftover meringues. You can store them in an airtight container for 1 to 2 days.

Calories 45	Total Fat 0 g	Cholesterol 0 mg	Total Carbohydrate 10 g	Protein 1 g
Calories from Fat 0	Saturated Fat 0 g	Sodium 15 mg	Dietary Fiber 1 g	Phosphorus 10 mg
	Trans Fat 0 g	Potassium 65 mg	Sugars 9 g	

SERVING SIZE 1 piece (1/8 of pie) | SERVES 8 | PREP/COOK TIME 15 minutes/55 minutes + cooling time
EXCHANGES for Pumpkin Pie: 3 Carbohydrate, 1 Fat
EXCHANGES for Maple Ginger Crust only: 1 1/2 Carbohydrate, 1/2 Fat

HOLIDAY PUMPKIN PIE WITH MAPLE GINGER CRUST

CRUST

- 1 1/2 cups graham-cracker crumbs (about 24 cracker squares)
- 3 tablespoons pure maple syrup
- 1 teaspoon canola oil
- 1 egg white, lightly beaten
- 1 teaspoon finely minced crystallized ginger
- 1/2 teaspoon ground ginger

FILLING

- 1/2 cup Splenda Sugar Blend
- 2 teaspoons ground cinnamon
- 1/2 teaspoon ground ginger
- 1/4 teaspoon ground cloves
- 1/4 teaspoon salt
- 2 eggs
- 1 teaspoon vanilla extract
- 1 (15-ounce) can pumpkin puree (not pumpkin pie filling)
- 1 teaspoon cornstarch
- 1 (12-ounce) can low-fat evaporated milk

GARNISH

- 1/2 cup fat-free whipped topping
- Zest of 1 fresh lemon

1 Preheat the oven to 425°F. In a bowl, combine all ingredients for the crust. Press into a 9-inch, nonstick pie pan, to form an even crust. Set aside.

2 In a bowl, mix together the Splenda, cinnamon, ginger, cloves, and salt.

3 In another bowl, beat the eggs and vanilla together. Add in the Splenda mixture and stir to combine.

4 Add in the pumpkin and stir until the mixture is well blended. Dissolve the cornstarch in about 2 to 3 tablespoons of the evaporated milk. Add the cornstarch mixture and the remaining evaporated milk to the pumpkin mixture, and mix until smooth. The mixture will be thin.

5 Pour the pumpkin pie filling into the prepared crust. Place the pie on a baking sheet. Bake for 15 minutes at 425°F. Lower the heat to 350°F, and bake an additional 40 minutes, or until the filling is set when a knife inserted comes out clean.

6 Remove the pie from the oven, and let cool for 2 hours before serving. Cut into 8 wedges. Top with whipped topping and sprinkle with lemon zest.

269

PUMPKIN PIE WITH MAPLE GINGER CRUST

Calories 255	Total Fat 5 g	Cholesterol 55 mg	Total Carbohydrate 46 g	Protein 7 g
Calories from Fat 45	Saturated Fat 1.4 g	Sodium 285 mg	Dietary Fiber 3 g	Phosphorus 165 mg
	Trans Fat 0 g	Potassium 340 mg	Sugars 32 g	

MAPLE GINGER CRUST ONLY

Calories 115	Total Fat 2.5 g	Cholesterol 0 mg	Total Carbohydrate 22 g	Protein 2 g
Calories from Fat 20	Saturated Fat 0.4 g	Sodium 135 mg	Dietary Fiber 1 g	Phosphorus 25 mg
	Trans Fat 0 g	Potassium 50 mg	Sugars 11 g	

MINI CHOCOLATE COFFEE ICE CREAM CUPS

8 ounces semisweet
    chocolate chips
1 cup light coffee ice cream
1/2 cup chocolate syrup

1 Melt the chocolate chips in a double boiler over simmering hot water until completely smooth.

2 Using the back of a teaspoon or a small spatula, coat the sides and bottom of small or mini silver foil paper baking cups with chocolate. Put the cups in 24 mini muffin pan wells.

3 Set the muffin pan trays in the refrigerator, and chill until the chocolate shells harden, approximately 30 to 45 minutes.

4 Once the shells are hardened, working quickly, evenly scoop the coffee ice cream into each shell. Drizzle with chocolate syrup, and serve immediately.

Calories 70	Total Fat 3 g	Cholesterol 0 mg	Total Carbohydrate 11 g	Protein 1 g
Calories from Fat 25	Saturated Fat 1.9 g	Sodium 10 mg	Dietary Fiber 1 g	Phosphorus 25 mg
	Trans Fat 0 g	Potassium 60 mg	Sugars 9 g	

DESSERTS

ARBORIO RICE AND FIG PUDDING

3/4 cup uncooked arborio rice

4 cups 1% milk

1/4 cup sugar

1/3 cup finely diced dried figs

1/2 teaspoon vanilla extract

Cinnamon for garnish

1 In a large, heavy pan, combine the rice, milk, and sugar. Bring to a gentle boil over high heat, lower the heat to medium, and continue to cook for 30 to 40 minutes. Stir frequently to prevent the rice from sticking to the bottom of the pan and to help release the starch from the rice. The mixture should be gently boiling the entire time; never let it come to a hard rolling boil. The rice should look very creamy, with a slight firmness but also cooked through. If you're serving the rice pudding cold, stop cooking when it still looks a bit runny. It will firm up as it chills in the refrigerator.

2 During the last 10 minutes of cooking, add in the figs (to serve the rice pudding cold, just add the figs when you finish cooking the rice entirely).

3 Remove the pan from the heat, and stir in the vanilla.

4 If serving the rice pudding warm, add 1/4 cup of the rice pudding to small dessert glasses. (Shot glasses work well; the pudding will pile high.) Dust the top of each serving with cinnamon, if desired. If serving the rice pudding cold, pour it from the pot into a bowl. Cover the surface of the pudding with plastic wrap (to prevent a skin from forming on the surface of the rice) and refrigerate for several hours. Proceed as above to fill the dessert glasses.

COOK'S TIP | When serving leftovers, add a bit of milk if the texture has become too firm.

Calories 100	**Total Fat 1 g**	**Cholesterol 5 mg**	**Total Carbohydrate 20 g**	**Protein 4 g**
Calories from Fat 10	Saturated Fat 0.5 g	**Sodium 35 mg**	Dietary Fiber 1 g	**Phosphorus 90 mg**
	Trans Fat 0 g	**Potassium 170 mg**	Sugars 11 g	

VERY GINGERY PUMPKIN MOUSSE

1 (1-ounce) package sugar-free, fat-free vanilla pudding mix (try also French vanilla or banana)

1 teaspoon ground cinnamon

1/2 teaspoon ground ginger

1/4 teaspoon ground nutmeg

1 1/2 cups cold 1% milk

1 cup pumpkin puree (not pumpkin pie filling)

1 cup fat-free whipped topping

3 gingersnap cookies, crushed into crumbs

2 tablespoons finely chopped crystallized ginger

1 In a large bowl, whisk together the dry vanilla pudding mix with the cinnamon, ginger, and nutmeg. Slowly whisk in the milk, whisking for 2 minutes. Add in the pumpkin, and continue to whisk until mixture begins to set. Fold in the whipped topping. Cover and refrigerate for 1 hour.

2 For each serving, put 1/4 cup of the pumpkin mousse in a dessert cup or dish. Add a layer of gingersnap crumbs. Add another 1/4 cup of the mousse on top of the crumbs. Sprinkle the top of each with 1 teaspoon chopped crystallized ginger.

275

Calories 105	Total Fat 1 g	Cholesterol 5 mg	Total Carbohydrate 21 g	Protein 3 g
Calories from Fat 10	Saturated Fat 0.6 g	Sodium 260 mg	Dietary Fiber 2 g	Phosphorus 200 mg
	Trans Fat 0 g	Potassium 205 mg	Sugars 12 g	

DESSERTS

PEAR AND CRANBERRY CAST-IRON CRISPS

CRUMB TOPPING

- 1/4 cup all-purpose flour
- 2 tablespoons granulated sugar
- 2 tablespoons light brown sugar
- 1/2 teaspoon cinnamon
- 1/4 teaspoon ground ginger
- 1/4 teaspoon ground nutmeg
  Pinch of salt
- 2 tablespoons nonhydrogenated margarine (such as Promise or Canoleo)
- 1 tablespoon chilled unsalted butter, cut into small bits

PEAR AND CRANBERRY FILLING

- 4 small (about 5 ounces each) Bosc or D'Anjou pears, peeled and chopped (about 3 cups)
- 1/4 cup dried cranberries
- 1/2 tablespoon sugar
- 2 teaspoons fresh lemon juice
- 1 teaspoon fresh lemon zest

- 2 tablespoons slivered almonds

1 Preheat the oven to 375°F. Coat two 6 1/2-inch cast-iron skillets with cooking spray. Set aside.

2 Prepare the topping: In a medium bowl, whisk together the flour, sugar, brown sugar, cinnamon, ginger, nutmeg, and salt. With a pastry blender or two knives, cut in the margarine and butter until coarse crumbs are formed. Set aside. You should have about 3/4 cup of topping.

3 For the pear and cranberry filling, mix together all the ingredients in a bowl. Divide the pear-cranberry mixture between the two cast-iron skillets, using about 1 1/2 cups of the mixture per skillet. Top the mixture with the crumb topping, dividing it evenly between the two skillets.

4 Put the skillets directly onto the oven rack, and bake uncovered for 20 minutes. Sprinkle the top of each crisp with the slivered almonds. Raise the heat to 400°F. Continue to bake the crisps for 5 minutes, or until the topping is light brown and crisp. Remove the crisps from the oven. You can serve directly from the skillets if desired.

Calories 180	Total Fat 6 g	Cholesterol 5 mg	Total Carbohydrate 31 g	Protein 1 g
Calories from Fat 55	Saturated Fat 2 g	Sodium 30 mg*	Dietary Fiber 2 g	Phosphorus 30 mg
	Trans Fat 0 g	Potassium 145 mg	Sugars 21 g	

*without added salt

CORN PUDDING

Butter-flavored cooking spray

3 slices center-cut bacon

2/3 cup diced onion

1 scallion, white part only, minced

1 garlic clove, minced

1 teaspoon sugar

Kosher salt and freshly ground black pepper to taste

Pinch crushed red pepper flakes

8 ounces frozen yellow corn, thawed and drained

3/4 cup 1% milk

1/4 cup yellow cornmeal

1 large egg

1/4 cup grated fresh Parmesan cheese

1 tablespoon fresh minced chive

1 Preheat the oven to 350°F. Coat 8 ramekin dishes (2-ounce size) with butter-flavored cooking spray. Set the ramekins inside a large rectangular baking dish. Set aside.

2 Add the bacon slices to a heavy skillet over medium-high heat. Cook the bacon on both sides until crisp. Remove the bacon from the skillet, drain on paper towels, and set aside.

3 Add the onion to the skillet, and sauté for 3 to 4 minutes. Add in the scallion and garlic, and sauté for 2 minutes. Add in the sugar, salt, pepper, and crushed red pepper, and sauté for 1 minute.

4 Add in the corn, and sauté for 2 minutes. Pour in the milk, lower the heat, and simmer for 4 minutes.

5 Ladle the corn mixture into a blender or food processor. Add in the cornmeal and egg, and process until smooth, leaving some texture.

6 Add the corn mixture to a bowl. Crumble the bacon into small pieces. Whisk in the bacon, Parmesan cheese, and chives. Divide the corn pudding among all the ramekin dishes. Pour hot water into the pan until the water comes halfway up the sides of the ramekin dishes.

7 Bake the puddings for about 40 minutes, or until set. A knife inserted in the center should come out clean.

9 Remove the pan from the oven, and let the puddings cool for about 5 minutes in the pan. With a set of firm tongs, carefully remove each ramekin from the water and serve.

COOK'S TIP | Using cornmeal will produce a pudding with a firm texture. For a more custardy pudding, substitute 1/4 cup all-purpose flour for the 1/4 cup cornmeal.

Calories 95	**Total Fat 3.5 g**	**Cholesterol 30 mg**	**Total Carbohydrate 12 g**	**Protein 5 g**
Calories from Fat 30	Saturated Fat 1.5 g	**Sodium 95 mg***	Dietary Fiber 1 g	**Phosphorus 105 mg**
	Trans Fat 0 g	**Potassium 160 mg**	Sugars 3 g	

*without added salt

FROZEN CRUNCHY PEANUT BUTTER PIE

1 quart fat-free vanilla ice cream, softened (such as Breyers Smooth & Dreamy)

1/4 cup crunchy natural peanut butter (such as Smucker's)

1 (9-inch) lower-fat graham cracker crust (such as Keebler Ready Crust Reduced Fat Graham Pie Crust)

1/4 cup chopped, roasted unsalted peanuts (or walnuts, pecans, or pistachios)

1/4 cup sugar-free chocolate syrup (such as Smucker's)

1 In a mixing bowl, use an electric mixer at medium-low speed to combine the softened ice cream and peanut butter.

2 Spread half of the mixture into the prepared crust. Sprinkle with half of the peanuts. Spread the remaining ice cream mixture on top. Sprinkle with the remaining peanuts. Drizzle the entire pie with chocolate syrup.

3 Freeze the pie for at least 6 hours, until firm. Remove the pie from the freezer about 10 minutes before serving. Use a knife warmed in hot water and wiped dry to make clean cuts.

281

Calories 235	**Total Fat 8 g**	**Cholesterol 0 mg**	**Total Carbohydrate 36 g**	**Protein 6 g**
Calories from Fat 70	Saturated Fat 1.6 g	**Sodium 140 mg**	Dietary Fiber 4 g	**Phosphorus 135 mg**
	Trans Fat 1.2 g	**Potassium 265 mg**	Sugars 8 g	

INDEXES

ALPHABETICAL INDEX

Note: Page numbers followed by *ph* refer to photographs.

SUBJECT INDEX

Note: Page numbers followed by *ph* refer to photographs.

288

his
worker

Suez
mobile